The
Musical
Imperative

by
Simon V. Anderson

Library of Congress
Catalog Card Number 83-73390

ISBN 0-915725-00-2

Copyright 1984 by the
Clifton Hills Press, Inc.
1034 Clifton Hills Avenue
Cincinnati, Ohio 45220

Typeset and Printed by
Capozzolo Typesetting and Printing
Cincinnati, Ohio

PROLOGUE

There must be forty books on the market for the basic music appreciation course in American undergraduate studies. Why write another one?

First, because the other books fail to treat the full musical environment with equal objectivity. Classical music gets generous coverage, but jazz, rock, Broadway, and country music suffer modest treatment by comparison.

Second, because most music appreciation books attempt too much. My students—500 or more each quarter term— have heavy schedules in their academic majors, and do not have time for those recommended indepth analyses of major classical works, not to mention the Suggestions for Further Listening, Additional Reading Sources, and the like. What my students need, and I think they are typical, is a tight, accurate, informative, objective survey of the musical options which lay out there beyond their current personal experiences.

Third, the other books put too much emphasis on "listening skills." People just don't listen to music the way most textbooks would seem to suggest—searching out areas of tension and resolution, identifying the changes of meter, recognizing differences in texture, and all the rest. People "feel" these things, of course, but nobody intellectualizes and verbalizes about them in the way we want our college students to. Even veteran concert-goers in classical and jazz circles would have a difficult time doing the things we ask our students to do in many of the music appreciation textbooks. It may be interesting to know about cadences, irregular metrical units, and disjunct melodic contours, but it is surely not critical for full musical "appreciation." We can enjoy a fine sirloin steak without any knowledge whatsoever of muscle fibers or the chemical properties of the meat. Nor is our pleasure greatly enhanced by learning the life and times of the cook who prepared the meal.

Fourth, all kinds of the wrong details are given in the other textbooks. Professors don't need a whole bundle of information about music—they're trained experts in the field. What they need are some new ideas on how to connect what they know so well to what their students ought to know. Students don't need pictures of trumpets and Renaissance paintings—these things are abundantly available elsewhere. What they need are some new ideas on how to connect what they know so well to what their professor seems to think they ought to know.

I have tried to make those connections, to offer many large observations on anything and everything related to the musical environment in modern America. I have presented a great variety of sweeping generalizations—many of them controversial, certainly unconventional—to open up some new thoughts on the "appreciation" of music. If I have succeeded, class discussions will get very interesting at times.

Fifth, and most important of all, the other music appreciation textbooks seem designed to try to change the musical tastes of the college students. This is a grave error, and nearly always fails. Musical taste—musical preference—is not a matter of knowledge, or generous exposure, or even serious study. It is a matter of family background, socioeconomic level, peer-group influences, self image (present and desired future), and many other strong and deeply rooted cultural circumstances. A few short hours of college study will surely not alter those preconditions.

Instruction should not be propaganda. Music appreciation books cannot "improve" or "raise" the musical activities of the land. Nor should they try. If, at the end of a music course, a student says, "No more Kenny Rogers and Barbara Mandrell for me. Nothing but Palestrina and Brahms for me from now on!" If this happens, the music course has been a total failure. We have merely replaced one kind of limitation with another.

Instead, at the end of the course, a student should be able to handle some of the basic terminology of the musical discipline, should be properly informed about the major styles, schools, forms, and such, and should be able to see the large picture of music as a form of specialized human behavior of a given crowd of people in a given historical time in a given location.

If this happens, the students will indeed have learned to "appreciate" music—to see what a potent force it is in the life of humankind, how diverse are its forms and styles, yet how consistent are its powers of fulfillment and enrichment. The basic purpose of a music appreciation course is not, after all, to persuade students that some kinds of music are better than others, but, rather, to show how all musical styles derive from and serve the same human needs and desires.

Yehudi Menuhin, conducting the Congress of Strings Orchestra during rehearsals in the Summer of 1983 at the College-Conservatory of Music, Cincinnati, Ohio. Courtesy of the CCM Publicity Office.

THE MUSICAL IMPERATIVE
TABLE OF CONTENTS

PART III: INSTRUMENTS AND INSTRUMENTAL FORMS

Part I
Introduction:
New Points
of View

1

Western Music

The music of Western Civilization makes sense to perhaps one-fifth of the people on earth: to the Germans, Scandinavians, British, French, North Americans, some of the Russians, and the many others in what is commonly called Occidental Civilization, or Western Culture. The remaining four-fifths of the inhabitants of the world—millions and millions of Chinese, Japanese, East Indians, Asiatic Russians, Australian and African blacks, North, South, and Central American Indians, Eskimos, South Sea Islanders, and hundreds of other ethnic groups—all these people would find the music of Western Culture totally meaningless because Western Music is outside their sociocultural frame of reference.

Four-fifths of humanity finds meaning, pleasure, and emotional release in musical systems which are profoundly different from music in Western Civilization. There simply is no such thing, for example, as harmony—in the Occidental sense—in the music of the Indians or the music of most Oriental cultures. Other cultures have simultaneous sounds in their music, to be sure, but not harmony. Not harmony, with its

ILLUSTRATION: Cincinnati Symphony Orchestra. Courtesy of the Cincinnati Symphony Orchestra.

gravitational pull toward a fixed tonal center. Not harmony, with its all-inclusive vertical and horizontal forces driving always toward, or away from, a given, or implied, nerve center.

Of course not. Occidental harmony grows out of the depths of a very special view of life. Out of the same psycho-emotional thrusts which produced the German Rothschild financial dynasty, the British Empire, General Motors, and BankAmerica. Occidental harmony derives from the same urges which resulted in Western kinship patterns, Judaic-Christian religious and legal doctrines, in the way the streets are outlined in Fargo, North Dakota, and in things like the Common Market and Little League Baseball. Occidental harmony is based on bedrock attitudes and assumptions about centrality, space, novelty, authority, goal-orientation, deferred gratification, time, and power.

The very act of "hearing" harmony is a cultural phenomenon of the highest subtlety. When someone plays C-E-G on the piano, Western listeners "hear" a "chord." An Alaskan Eskimo fisherman might not. He might hear a composite glob of sound, without definition of any kind. There really are not three distinct and separate tones being produced, but only a singular acoustical disturbance which the Western Mind has learned to interpret in a specific manner. When Leonard Bernstein hears a symphony orchestra "move" from one chord to another, he is engaged in an act of special cultural conditioning. And when Buck Owens hears his steel guitar player "move" from one chord to another, he too is engaged in a culturally conditioned response of enormous complexity and refinement. And neither Bernstein's nor Buck Owens' experience would make any sense, whatsoever, to four-fifths of humanity.

Likewise with Western melody, rhythm, form, scales, instruments, singing styles, and the way symphony orchestras are arranged on a concert stage. These musical appointments give shape and substance to the most profound and persistent implicit and explicit concepts of Western Culture, of the Atlantic Civilization, as it is now called by some scholars. Aaron Copland's idea of what a melody ought to be is fundamentally different from a Japanese koto performer's concept of

4

what a melody ought to be, and this difference derives from and reveals a fundamentally different psychoemotional approach to life.

Each culture operates within its own very special view of reality and with its own very special feeling for space, time, territoriality, play, authority, and all the other components in what Anthropologist Edward T. Hall calls the "vocabulary of culture."[1] Cultures do interlace, of course, and they do leave their mark on each other. But the fact that symphony orchestras are on the increase in Japan does not mean that the Japanese have finally seen the light. It means, simply, that Japan is becoming Westernized at certain deep levels of its society: the Japanese are also abandoning ancient traditions of honoring and caring for their elders, baseball is getting to be big business, and their industrial development has become the envy of the world.

While other countries are watching Japan leap into the 20th century, Western Civilization has gone through a blinding storm of art styles, schools, periods, and aesthetic creeds. In the days of old, schools of aesthetic consistency (Baroque, Classic, Romantic, and such) were long range time periods. In the 20th century, with time compressed through instantaneous communication, aesthetic schools come and go in a few short years: primitivism, futurism, folklorism, cubism, abstract expressionism, surrealism, aleatoric music, the theater of the absurd, pop art, op art, junk-metal sculpture, ambient music, and whole schools of nostalgia in all the classical and popular arts—all these things have come and gone, and are still here. These are bewildering days when nearly all the arts of the historical past and all the artistic experiments of the historical present are somewhere available for examination and participation.

What this means, of course, is that the fundamental assumptions of Western Society are in a state of continuous adjustment, modification, and mutation. In his highly entertaining *Future Shock*[2], Alvin Toffler uses terms like "throwaway culture," "new nomads," "modular man," "experience makers," "overchoice," and "life style factories" to suggest just how transient and diverse Western life styles have become. His

5

Third Wave[3] is even more provocative, for he boldly asserts that just as the First Wave (agricultural society) was washed away by the Second Wave (industrial society), a Third Wave (called different things by different writers: the Space Age, Electronic Era, Post-Industrial Society, the Silicone Scene) is rapidly washing away all the Second Wave attitudes and principles.

For all the diversity and continuous change in Western Culture, it is still a remarkably uniform society which is easily recognized as being substantially different from other major cultures. This music appreciation book will examine the special musical behavior of this special culture. The West.

READING NOTES FOR CHAPTER ONE

[1]Edward T. Hall, *The Silent Language* (Greenwich, Conn.: Fawcett Publications, Inc., 1959), Chapter Three, "The Vocabulary of Culture," pp. 42-62.

[2]Alvin Toffler, *Future Shock* (New York: Random House, 1970). The term, "future shock," found its way into America's vocabulary immediately after the appearance of Toffler's book.

[3]Alvin Toffler, *The Third Wave* (New York: William Morrow and Co., Inc., 1980).

2

The Best
In The
West

Music appreciation courses are concerned with classical music. They should be. This body of music represents the towering achievement of some of the most sophisticated and inspired musicians in Western Culture. The magnificent works of Palestrina, Beethoven, Stravinsky, and others quite properly rank with the pyramids, the Parthenon, and the Notre Dame Cathedral as examples of the highest level of artistic creation. Music did not get better after Beethoven, it got different. Beethoven is, and always will be, worth studying because his music is absolutely the best of its kind.

Classical music is not the only story, however, and there are other peaks in the musical behavior of the West—like the musical score to *Oklahoma*, for example, and the now famous Benny Goodman Concert at Carnegie Hall in 1938—each a unique moment in the history of its genre, and each absolutely the best of its kind.

The omission of country music, jazz, and other popular styles from many music appreciation courses comes from a belief by some college teachers that popular music is not an art, and, therefore, not appropriate material for academic study.

ILLUSTRATION: Harpsichord, by Joseph Kirkman, London, 1798
(Boston Museum of Fine Arts)

A new age is taking shape, though, and whether it is art or not, popular music is being taught more and more often these days—right along with Financial Planning for the Single Parent, Suburban Lawn Care, and Advanced Macrame. Nearly all interests and skills are available for college study today. Indeed, Glenn Campbell was recently appointed adjunct professor of music at UCLA.

QUESTION: WHAT IS ART?

Just what is art, after all? If art captures the imagination and gives form and substance to the most profound assumptions and aspirations of a society; if art brings self-revelation in ways no other communicative gesture can; if art delights the senses and nourishes the soul; if art stimulates an individual to new levels of awareness; if art is all this and more—as the literature of the philosophers and aestheticians would suggest—if all this is the case, then Willie Nelson's treatment of "You Were Always On My Mind" just might be art. And Duke Ellington's "Sophisticated Lady."

For many years Western Society made a great effort to establish a distinction between "major" and "minor" arts, that is, between the "fine" arts and "utilitarian" arts, with a higher aesthetic value assigned to the "fine" arts. And even today, writers call certain things "pop" art to distinguish them from the other stuff, real art. And students study "commercial art" which is decidedly a different curriculum from the other, pure art, baccalaureate program of studies.

In the literature on music, the term "serious music" was common for a long time, meaning classical music, sometimes called art music, occasionally fine art music, as being distinct from folk music, popular music, Broadway show tunes, jazz, and other things. The term "serious" has almost disappeared from modern writing, though, because it seems to suggest that Duke Ellington might not have been serious about his music, and that Richard Rodgers' score to *Oklahoma* should not be considered as a serious artistic effort. Such thoughts do not sit well with Americans today, at all.

Some people simply avoid the decision as to what is of *art* quality and what is not. *Billboard* carries the following categories: Classical, Top-40, Soul, Country, Adult Contemporary, Jazz, Disco, Latin, Gospel, and Rock. The *Schwann Record and Tape Guide* lists Jazz, Popular, Classical, and a composite category called Musicals-Movies-TV. ASCAP (The American Society of Composers, Authors, and Publishers) has two broad divisions, Standard and Popular. The first covers symphonic, chamber, and educational music. The second covers jazz, films, pop-rock, country and western, rhythm and blues, and musical theater.

The whole problem of what is art and what is not art hangs on the issue of aesthetic value. Judaic-Christian Culture has always assigned higher aesthetic value to certain forms of behavior over other forms of closely related behavior. Ballet, for example, was art, while gymnastics and figure skating were sport. Opera singers were artists; Bing Crosby was an entertainer. String quartets were art, radio jingles were not. And for a long time America suffered an inferiority complex in artistic things, favoring European derived art products over native American art products. The American things did not seem to have a high enough aesthetic value for serious consideration. The whole idea of aesthetic value has been masterfully explored by Alan Merriam in his *Anthropology of Music* where he establishes quite convincingly that "aesthetic value" is a notion peculiar to only certain cultures.[1] The natives of Bali have no word for "art." They do everything as well as they can.[2]

Part of the problem with the categories of different levels of aesthetic value (artistic significance) lies in the strange attitude so evident in Western Culture, especially in America. For all the lip service paid to the arts—to the profound beauty and eternal value of, say, ballet or opera—not many American fathers would be pleased if a ten-year-old son should one day announce, "Dad, I want to be a ballet dancer." Or, "Dad, I want to be a poet." And it would not be just the rigors and financial insecurity of a career in ballet which would give the typical American father reason for pause. The father's reluctance would come from a deep seated suspicion that opera and ballet and poetry are somehow not central to what life is and ought to be all about.

9

The history of American Culture shows a kind of ambivalence toward the arts, and most fathers and mothers would feel much more comfortable if their son said that he would continue his cello lessons, yes, but he planned to go into the field of business, or law, or that he wanted to be a building contractor.

An interesting case can be built if the hypothesis is made that the arts are, in fact, central to existence, but that American society has failed to recognize the arts in their diverse forms. Where is America's real ballet, for example? Where is the ultimate, the highest, form of graceful bodily movement? Where are those nearly unbelievable feats of timing, strength, poise, endurance, effortless beauty in form, function, and style? Where is that display of intense concentration which quickens the heart, and captures the spirit of what it is to be an American, which gives substance to all the nuances and overtones of the National Anthem? Where is the real American ballet?

Perhaps it is on the NBA Game of the Week, with "Dr. J.," Julius Erving, leaping toward the basket in the most astonishing demonstration of physical grace and style American society can offer. It might be in Dorothy Hamill's kind of poetry in motion. It might be that Tom Seaver, Kareem Abdul-Jabbar, and Tony Dorsett are America's new ballet artists, served up on the electronic stage of the television screen. And the instant slow motion replays reward and reveal so much that some sports fans now carry small television sets to the games so they can watch the slo-mo sequences even while sitting in the stadium. Several large sports complexes now have giant six-sided television screens hung from the center of the arena.

Maybe America is in the process of developing a new form of ballet to complement the traditional European form. Some athletes are taking ballet lessons, and finding it quite helpful. And a few years ago, Edward Villella, principal dancer with the New York City Ballet, presented Tom Seaver, Jerry Grote, Virginia Wade, George McGinnis, Bob Griese, and Muriel Grossfield in a CBS Special, "Dance of the Athletes." The TV special compared the athleticism shared by sports figures and dancers. Against a background of original music, the graceful and fluid motions of the athletes appeared as a special kind of "ballet." Some of the athletes have since retired, but the program made its point.

Where is America's genuine opera? Where is that poetic-dramatic vehicle which brings to the surface all the most cherished myths of the tribe? That form of musical theater which derives from, and speaks to, the unique character of American society? That total theater which gives America an increased level of self awareness? That does for the Americans what *Rigoletto* does for the Italians? That does for the Americans what *Tristan and Isolde* does for the Germans? Perhaps it is *Oklahoma*, for some, the Grand Ole Opry, for others, and *The Wiz*, for others.

Perhaps America is too spread out—geographically and genetically—to come up with a unified and consistent musical style period like, say, the Viennese Classical School. With its unusual ethnic diversity and enormous stretches of land, America may never produce anything quite like the period of French Impressionism. But America has its own way of doing things. How about Motown, and Chicago Dixieland in the 1920s, and The Nashville Sound?

Some scholars believe that America has its own aesthetic doctrines, but since the American art forms are different from traditional art forms, the American art forms get no respect—the Hollywood musical, McDonalds' architecture, the daytime (and now prime time) soap opera, the classic gangster movie, the Saturday morning cartoons, and such. A whole new scholarly discipline is available now in university graduate schools—the study of American popular culture. Learned treatises are being written on the comic strips, the TV commercial, science fiction, the cowboy movie, and similar topics. The TV lounges of many college dormitories and Greek houses are packed daily with students intently following their favorite soap opera. A Chicago high school teacher uses scripts and notes on *Happy Days* as a textbook for a course in adolescent psychology.

What this all means, of course, is that the traditional definitions and delimitations of artistic and scholarly endeavors are changing.

To return to music. Many music appreciation books concentrate on classical music over other styles because of a firm belief that only the best music should be studied in an educational setting. Of course. But "best" by what measure of value? Best on whose judgment? Is an operatic aria, by that very fact, better than a country blues tune? Is a movement from a symphony better, by that very fact alone, than an overture to a Broadway show? Would the world be better if Duke Ellington had been a concert pianist instead of a jazz musician?

Of course not. Music is music, and it occurs at different levels—social, economic, emotional, psychological. If "Amazin' Grace" moves a large congregation to tears of joy, surely those tears are not any less valuable as a human experience than similar tears of joy produced in a different congregation by Handel's "Hallelujah" chorus.

Music is one of the arts. And just what are the arts? This is the critical question. If the arts are clearly understood, the arts appreciation courses all over America can address themselves to the job at hand with increased skill and precision. If the arts are not clearly understood, the arts appreciation courses become tools of propaganda for one generation or one social level to foist off on to another a preconceived set of observations and attitudes. There is quite a bit of this in all education, of course, and there should be. No need for each generation to go through the trials and errors of earlier generations.

But the arts are different from physics. The law of gravity is the same for all ethnic cultures and all generations. But not what is "beautiful" or "good" or "pleasurable." These are different "realities" for different ethnic groups and generations and socioeconomic levels.

ANSWER: ART IS COMMUNICATION THROUGH SYMBOLS.

Every culture casts up its most intense and eloquent statements on the eternal mysteries and beauties of existence—on life, death, love, fear, anger, solitude, ambition, pleasure, pain, and such. These statements are delivered through manipulations of time, sound, visual impressions, touch, language, space, bodily movement, and other communicative gestures which are so common to the culture that the senders and receivers agree, consciously and subconsciously, on the vocabulary, grammar, and syntax of the symbolic language of the art form. That's it.

This is what "art" is, what the "arts" are. Glorious and powerful expressions of the deepest human attitudes possible.

Most of these art forms were utilitarian at one time, some still are, like architecture. Music, for instance, may have originated in mating calls, or in noises shouted to frighten away predators, or in the need for a special kind of communication among the members of an early tribe. Whatever its origin, music immediately took on a life of its own, and assumed the position of a cultural imperative. All known societies, past and present, have had and now have some kind of music—hence the title of this book, *The Musical Imperative*.

Just as different ethnic groups, different races, different socioeconomic levels within various societies, even different generations within a given society, have their own manners of speech, dress, entertainment, humor, interpersonal associations and the like—so, too, are they drawn to produce and consume their own special musical style. A style which has cultural currency for them, with its own standards of quality, value, meaningfulness, and aesthetic significance. Mozart is remembered over Ditters von Dittersdorf because Mozart was a much better composer. Jimi Hendrix rose to the top because he was far more talented and creative than hundreds of other rock guitarists.

Brahms and Basie and Buck Owens are different because they grow in different sociocultural soil. To call one "classical" and another "jazz" and the other "country" simply puts labels on the misunderstanding. Better to dig into the sociocultural terrain, a bit, to see what lies below the turf, hidden from view.

One of the buried nuggets is a cultural concept of time. Among many other things, the handling of time in a musico-aesthetic sense helps to explain some of the fundamental differences between and among the various forms of musical behavior in the land.

13

READING NOTES FOR CHAPTER TWO

[1] Alan P. Merriam, *The Anthropology of Music* (Evanston, Illinois: Northwestern University Press, 1964), pp. 259-76.

[2] Merriam's *Anthropology*, above, is the single most important book about musical behavior to have been written in the 20th century.

3

The Voice Of Time

In *The Silent Language*, Edward T. Hall, anthropologist, examines time as a cultural factor.[1] He shows how different cultures handle time. Europeans and Americans treat it like a continuous ribbon, measured and blocked out in units which a are consumed according to schedules and appointments. Time is linear, sequential, and a precious commodity to be spent carefully and regulated consciously. But Latin Americans, Navajo Indians, Orientals, and many other societies do not hold to this same kind of punctual-compulsive sense of time. Their sense of time is quite different. Time, for many other cultures, is an endless unfolding of the natural rhythms of life. Or, a "museum with endless corridors and alcoves." A total experiencing of the vivid Now. Things begin and end when the feeling is right, not when the clock or appointment calendar dictates. This different concept of time leads to major misunderstandings between American government officials and their counterparts in non-Western governments.

Anthropologists have learned that the same kind of problem often occurs between social levels of the same culture.

ILLUSTRATION: Eugene Ormandy, Conductor. Courtesy of CBS Records.

In America, for example, time is handled differently by the three major socioeconomic classes—the upper class, the middle class, and the lower class.[2] Especially at the bottom half of the lower class, there seems to be no organization of behavior through time toward goals.

Consider, now, that two of America's major popular music styles, jazz and country music, have their roots in poverty-level society, and some important contrasts reveal themselves between music born in one class level versus another. Indeed, not only music, but all the arts.

At the upper levels of society the arts give form to very special concepts of the organization of expressive behavior, through time, toward aesthetic goals. The arts grow out of finely cultivated patterns of deferred gratification, that is, out of a capacity for delayed reward, because experience shows that things work out nicely for those members of the upper classes who put their immediate needs on hold until the appropriate time for satisfaction. *Macbeth* and a Beethoven symphony develop through an organic curve best diagrammed as an arc, with the intense peak coming, quite often, about two-thirds or more of the way through the whole aesthetic experience.

Of course. This arc is the general shape of life at the higher socioeconomic levels—with the peak experience being college graduation for the last child or that long-sought promotion to board membership in the corporation or firm.

In specific musical terms, this arc materializes out of complex chord structures and key relationships which build toward a peak, out of linear, goal-oriented melodies derived from motives eager for elaboration and fulfillment, and out of sounds and gestures which lead to architectural forms. The music mirrors all those middle and upper class virtues of control, reserve, long range planning, emotional growth, goal orientation, and purposeful drive. The whole musical art emerges as a kind of continuous "process of becoming," in preparation for a glorious denouement.

The arts in the lower levels of society, on the other hand, give form to a completely different state of affairs. Deferred gratification is no great virtue, here. All evidence and experience show that things never have worked out, and probably never will work out, and only a fool would wait around to be done in by the Establishment again. Anthropologist Jules Henry once used the term "survival-self culture," and explained that members of a survival-self culture focus their energies on activities which give them continuous and vivid reassurance that they are alive. What kind of art works come from such cultures?

Country music, jazz, gospel, rock, and blues are multi-million dollar industries now, but they were born in poverty-level, survival-self, cultures. Their musical organic line is best diagrammed as a spiral, with no specific long range peak goal, but, instead, a continuous exploration of a fixed and very intense and vivid psychoemotional station. No broadly conceived long range aesthetic operation here, but, rather, a program of vigorously cultivated patterns of pulsating rewards, similar to what James Joyce called "epiphanies"—episodes of cumulative revelation.

Of course. This spiral is the general shape of poverty level life, with no long planned goals ever coming into realization, with job changes frequent and unpredictable, with life being full of short term, closed experiences, with no hope of ever being promoted to a position of real security and prestige.

In specific musical terms, this spiral materializes out of simple chord structures and fixed tonal centers which turn upon themselves in recurring non-developing sensuous-pleasurable sonorities, out of short and uncomplicated stock formula melodic materials that are rich in themselves and little concerned with elaboration, and out of sounds and gestures which work themselves out in direct non-architectural forms. No upper class virtues of long range planning, deferred gratification, and all that kind of thing here. The whole musical art emerges as a kind of continuous, straight-forward, open "declaration of being."

Now the critical component, here, is the sense of time, and this sense of time determines how melody, harmony, rhythm, and the other musical materials will take shape and functional operation in the music of a given subculture. Two important considerations obtain in regard to this most basic fact.

First, there is no relationship between aesthetic value and the sense of time which is at work in the music: there are good symphonies and bad symphonies, there is good jazz and bad jazz, there is good country music and bad country music, there are good oratorios and bad oratorios. The aesthetic value or "quality" of a given musical endeavor must be judged in each case on the success or effectiveness of the endeavor itself, on its own unique terms, within the frame of its own reference. No amount of time-honored classical tradition will make a bad art song better than a good pop tune.

Second, this sense of time thing is terribly complex and confusing. Count Basie and Ray Charles came out of poverty-level circumstances. So did Merle Haggard and Johnny Cash. These musicians are wealthy international superstars now, however, with schedules and appointments and TV commitments—still they work in the musical system which makes emotional sense to them. Meanwhile, symphony orchestra musicians, making much less financially than Johnny Cash, will spend their whole lives in a musical system which fits their emotional and intellectual sense of what music is and ought to be. There are wealthy and poor symphony musicians and fans; there are wealthy and poor country musicians and fans.

There seems to be a consistent sense of time throughout a given musical enterprise, though. Jazz and rock concerts often start an hour late and run two hours beyond the stated program time, while symphony concerts begin promptly at 8:30 p.m. and end when they are supposed to. Gospel sing-outs and barbershop reviews go on until the early morning hours, while piano recitals and chamber concerts are nearly always over by 10:30 p.m. Very little at all happens at all in Nashville until noon, but symphony orchestras have 9:30 a.m. rehearsals as routine procedure.

To repeat, this sense of time is terribly complex and confusing. Suffice to say that the consistent factor among symphony subscribers, or jazz aficionados, or Blue Grass buffs, is more likely to be in the way they handle time in their lives than it is in the current specific level of their socioeconomic circumstances. Or perhaps it is more accurate to say that the consistent factor is in the way the performers and audiences handle time throughout this specific sociocultural ritual. Symphony performers and audiences gather together in a manner in which the whole ritual, the music especially, demonstrates a sense of time that is rigorously controlled and judiciously consumed according to careful plans. Jazz and rock performers and audiences gather together in a manner in which the whole ritual, the music especially, demonstrates a sense of time that is casually manipulated and consumed according to the ebb and flow of the collective mood of all parties to the experience.

There are many other differences between and among the various musical styles in American society. The sounds produced by different performers on the same instruments, for instance, reveal deep feelings and ideals. Jazz clarinet tone, as opposed to the classical clarinet tone, for example. And Louis Armstrong's trumpet sound, as compared with the sound of a traditional symphony trumpet player. What is a desired tone color for one culture may be highly undesirable for another culture. Imagine Andre Segovia at an Eric Clapton concert.

There are many sounds and gestures which make jazz and rock different from Beethoven and Bartok, then. Among the most significant, though, is the subtle manner in which each of the major musical styles works out its own persuasive rhetoric and speaks to its creators and consumers in its own special voice of time.

READING NOTES FOR CHAPTER THREE

[1]Edward T. Hall, *The Silent Language*, (Greenwich, Conn.: Fawcett Publications, Inc., 1959), Chapter One, pp. 15-30.

[2]An excellent summary of the various social classes in America can be found in Ian Robertson, *Sociology* (New York: Worth Publishers, Inc., 1977), Chapter Eleven, "Social Class in the United States," pp. 237-259.

The
Meaning
Of
Music

Generally speaking, there are two great schools of opinion on the meaning of music: (1) the Absolutists believe that music has no intrinsic meaning whatsoever, that what is understood or felt as meaning is nothing more than an emotional response to the stimulating pleasure of the sounds and a kind of satisfying joy in the organizational order of the total experience; and (2) the Referentialists believe that music represents, or refers to, in some vague way, certain extra-musical states of being—like happiness, or sadness, or love, or rage, or comfort, or whatever. A good number of subschools exist (Abstract Formalism, Abstract Expressionism, Social Realism, Symbolism, and others), each armed with loaded philosophical and scholarly weapons to gun down the others, and establish, once and for all, full and secure control of the territory of aesthetic meaning.[1] The literature of the music profession is flooded with learned treatises which analyze, describe, and finally define musical meaning as this or that or the other thing.

ILLUSTRATION: Orchestral musicians at rehearsal. College-Conservatory of Music, University of Cincinnati. Courtesy of the CCM Publicity Office.

All the major poets and philosophers have discussed music.[2] Plato believed that music could refine the character and preserve good health, but that too much music could cause a man's character to be "melted and softened beyond what is good." Aristotle believed that the aim of art was purification. Music was especially good at drawing off unsocial and destructive impulses into harmless excitement. But Aristotle, too, cautioned that too much music was a dangerous thing. Augustine confessed, among other things, "to have sinned criminally . . . by being more moved by the singing than by what is sung." He thought music had its place, though, because "by the delights of the ear, the weaker minds may be stimulated to a devotional frame."

Schopenhaur believed that music was the most powerful of all the arts, because it could most immediately and powerfully elevate man above the strife of Will. Goethe is supposed to have said that architecture was "frozen music." Henri Bergson considered musical works to be "records of intuitions." Freud believed that music was a sublimation process in which the composer converts his repressions and unfulfilled wishes into tonal fantasies expressing his desires. Charles Darwin believed that music preceded the existence of articulate speech, and was used originally as a factor in attracting and selecting a mate.

All this scholarly and philosophical footwork is interesting and entertaining to be sure. The blunt truth is, however, that music is simply a form of social behavior through which a given crowd of people exchange and reaffirm attitudes they hold in common. No more; no less. But that's enough. Enough to be a critical activity in the life of all non-industrial societies, and enough to be a major industry in every industrial society.

Music is a highly specialized social behavior, as is every language of communication, of course. Edward Sapir and his student Benjamin Whorf hypothesized 50 years ago that different languages reveal distinctly different worlds, not just different terms for the same world. Leonard Bernstein drew heavily on this philosophy in his *Unanswered Question*.

Such is the power of language—spoken, musical, or body—that gross misinterpretation often occurs by someone outside the culture. A raised eyebrow means one thing in one culture, but something quite different in another. Body odors are welcome in some cultures, and marriage matchmakers smell the prospective bride and groom to determine if they will be compatible. Such is just not the case in Western Civilization.

Likewise with music. A throbbing tenor saxophone is much in demand in jazz, but somehow totally out of place in a Mozart symphony. And the reverse. An operatic voice is glorious in opera, but ludicrous in jazz. On a less obvious level, a rich E-flat augmented eleventh chord is absolutely right for a certain moment in a Duke Ellington tune, but the same chord would destroy Willie Nelson's "Blue Eyes Cryin' In The Rain." In fact the superimpostion of one musical gesture on another musical culture is so shocking and humorous that Peter Schickele, the promoter of the works of "P. D. Q. Bach," has made a successful career in comedy by doing just that.

If music had meaning separate from the cultural matrix of its origin, that meaning would come from the combined meaning of the pieces and components—chords, rhythms, melodic intervals, etc.—which go to make up the whole. Thus, a certain chord would mean the same thing whether in jazz or country music or opera.

But no. Every musical style has its own inner laws which make it what it is. Even mixing periods within a major style category does not work. To put a Romantic crescendo and cymbal crash in a Bach cantata would be criminal. But what a glorious effect that gesture is in Tchiakovsky. To throw a Dixieland lick into a be-bop setting never works at all, but what a happy event that same Dixieland tail-gate trombone line is the way Jack Teagarden did it in the 1920s.

The real "meaning" of music defies verbalization, of course, as much as the real meaning of love, or friendship, or joy, or sorrow. Yet music conveys something very specific and accurate from the performers to the listeners. The study of just what it is that music conveys between and among its performers and audiences has consumed the intellectual and scholarly energies of Alan Lomax, now, for over 20 years.

Lomax, folklorist and musical scholar with an anthropologist's eye and ear, has developed an elaborate system of "cantometrics," roughly, the study of the relationships between song style and life style. His findings show promise of enormous insights into music as a form of human behavior. He has recorded, catalogued, and analyzed the main song styles of every known major ethnic group. The raw information has been codified and compared with information drawn from the *Ethnographic Atlas* (Murdock, 1962-67) which provides standardized ethnographic ratings for subsistence type, family kinship patterns, settlement types, political organization, etc. Norman Berkowitz supervised the procedures of programming, classification, and retrieval of information at the Columbia University Computer Center.

Summarizing his findings in *Folk Song Style and Culture* (1968), Lomax opened up some exciting areas of thinking about the reasons for differences in musical styles:

(1) In general, song styles from complex cultures are dense with information, while songs from simple economies carry less information load (page 128).

(2) Where feminine premarital sexual activity is restricted or severely sanctioned, narrowing and nasality, both signs of tension, become prominent and constant features of the culture's singing style (pages 195-96).

(3) Rhythmic interplay, rhythmic counterpoint, plays a large part in the music of cultures which are complex in political organization (page 68).[3]

Lomax's book is a gold mine of information which shows how consistent certain musical circumstances are with given conditions in a specific sociocultural matrix. There are forty-four more correlations like the three listed above, each explaining how music reveals, reflects, and reinforces the attitudes, beliefs, and habits of that society. Lomax has enlisted the aid of recognized scholars in the analysis and interpretation of the mountains of raw data he has gathered, and he presents only those conclusions which surface at the highest levels of statistical significance.

Lomax's monumental research studies lead to a perfectly clear understanding—perhaps for the first time in the history of aesthetics—of what music really means, or, better, what music really does in the life of humankind. At the risk of oversimplification, a summary paragraph or two will serve to encapsule Lomax's views on music, and will serve also as a fitting conclusion to this first section of *The Musical Imperative*.

Music is a form of learned behavior. It does not exist outside, or separate from, the human experience. All human experiences derive meaning from and leave residual effects on the peculiar culture of their origin. Music is no more mysterious than facial expressions, clothing, or any other of the wonderfully diverse circumstances which mark one culture as being different from another culture.

The beautiful poetic declarations of Plato, Aristotle, Goethe, and the other philosophers notwithstanding, Western music serves to celebrate Western philosophical beliefs just like Navajo music celebrates the way of life among the Navajo Indians. Specifically, Judaic-Christian Western Culture with its monotheistic concept of religion comes to tonality rather easily and comfortably—tonality as a musical value (for a long time, at least). What a beautiful metaphor for the collective Western Mind is a Beethoven symphony: conquering all obstacles, bringing order out of chaos, rising triumphantly in architectural strength and linear logic over all disrupting influences to settle finally in glorious victory on the powerful hammer strokes of the God-given tonic chord.

Other cultures have different ideas of what musical joy is and ought to be because they live by different psycho-emotional drives. Likewise, within a large major culture, different musical styles come from the different subcultures. Thus country music, jazz, classical music, Broadway, Tex-Mex, rock, rhythm and blues, and all the other styles give shape and substance to the subtly but profoundly different attitudes and habits which characterize America's various subcultures.

The Musical Imperative will, then, sweep over the major styles of the music of America's major subcultures to examine the great moments in the history of those styles. The purpose of the book is to open musical doors which might not otherwise get opened. The heaviest door, the door most difficult to open, is, of course, the door to classical music. This book will, therefore, spend a bit more time putting oil on the hinges of that door than on some of the other doors. Not because opening the door to classical music will lead to some kind of Better Land of Musical Awareness, but just because that door is harder to open than the other doors.

If this book is successful, the final judgment of the students ought to be something like this, "I still like _____ music, of course, but isn't it really marvelous how the same satisfaction I need and get from my favorite music is available to my fellow citizens in their music, the music of _____ ." Fill in your own blanks, and move on now to Part II of *The Musical Imperative*.

READING NOTES FOR CHAPTER FOUR

[1]The best quick summary of the various philosophies on the meaning of music is Bennett Reimer, *A Philosophy of Music Education* (Englewood Cliffs, New Jersey: Prentice-Hall, Inc., 1970), Chapter Two, "Alternative Views About Art," pp. 12-27.

[2]An excellent source for the thoughts of famous people about music Nat Shapiro (compiler), *an Encyclopedia of Quotations About Music* (New York: Da Capo Press, 1978).

[3]Alan Lomax, *Folk Song Style and Culture* (Washington, D.C.: American Association for the Advancement of science, 1968).

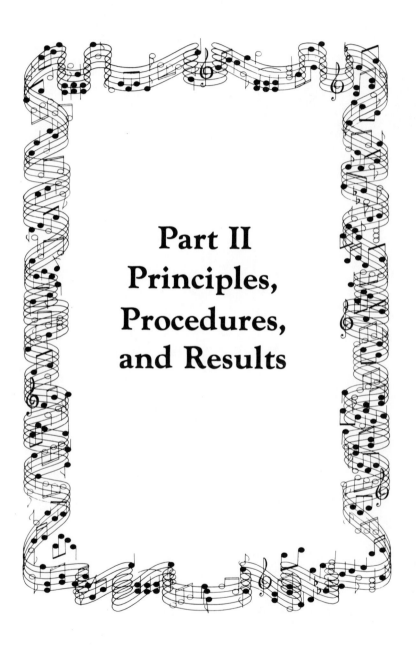

Part II
Principles,
Procedures,
and Results

Common Components in the Music of Western Civilization

For all the diversity of musical styles among the various subcultures in Western Civilization, there are certain musical ingredients, or components, which clearly mark this music as different from Oriental, or African, or Indian musical systems. Western music—all the way from German symphonies to English operettas to Broadway and jazz—takes shape and substance out of six common components: (1) tone, (2) rhythm, (3) melody, (4) harmony, (5) texture, and (6) expressive devices. These common components arise from a much deeper common approach to life. Hughson Mooney makes the point dramatic.

> *The cultural origins of Westerners are partly Biblical. We are fiercely apocalyptic, habitually exhilarated and exalted by millenarian visions, then depressed when we cannot achieve them. Our "modernized" or*

ILLUSTRATION: Miles Davis at Carnegie Hall. The legendary performance of May 19, 1961. Courtesy of CBS Records.

"liberated" men and women may of course seek not the Holy Grail, per se, but a better orgasm or a new Society. Nevertheless, they go about their searchings with the intensity of the Hebrews struggling for their millenium.

Despite many new ways of saying old things, 1970 rock was of a piece with the Protestant hymns of the 1870s, the Old Testament Jeremiahs, to say nothing of such 1920s songs, such as "I'm Sitting on Top of the World," or "I'm on the Crest of a Wave"—all timeless expressions of Western moods.

The last two, for instance, while they may particularly reveal something about people just before the great market crash, express more fundamentally something about Westerners throughout history—an almost hallucinatory Judaeo-Christian anthropocentrism as old as the story of creation and as recent as the Burt Bacharaach-Hal David "New World" (1970), or the Jefferson Airplane's "Crown of Creation."

We will not tolerate their obstruction, sang the Airplane in 1968. So sang the Old Testament of smoting the Philistines hip and thigh, and with the same Western sense of a morally manifest destiny. The very words of such songs would have no meaning to classical Hindu, Buddhist, Taoist, or Confucian. Untouched by the sort of humanism peculiar to the West, Oriental sages would find ridiculously deluded any assumption that sitting on top of the world, climbing the highest mountain (to paraphrase a 1926 title), and saying, "We want the world, and we want it now," could ever change, much less perfect, the universe.

The entire gamut of Western musical expression from the Te Deum down through Handel's Messiah to Vincent Youman's "Hallelujah" and to the apocalyptic protest ballad of the 1960s—all this is of a piece with the trumpet of Jericho, with tales told by the tribesmen who believed that God had parted the waves of the Red Sea and held back the sun at Jericho so that His children could have their world and have it now.[1]

The Jefferson Airplane, later the Jefferson Starship, comes and goes into and out of existence frequently these days, but otherwise Mooney's colorful remarks hold up well. Judaic-Christian Culture is something special, indeed. A special view of reality. A unique conception of what life is, and ought to be, all about. Out of this distinct approach to life comes an equally distinct musical language, different from the musical language of other cultures. Western Music—whether jazz, or country music, or classical music, or whatever—derives from six basic common components.

TONE

The first and most obvious thing about music is that it is made up of some kind of acoustical disturbance, sound, as it is called, or in musical parlance, "tone." Acousticians and musicians talk about four characteristics of sound:

ACOUSTICS	MUSIC
1. Frequency	1. Pitch
2. Amplitude	2. Dynamic Level
3. Harmonic Constitution	3. Timbre (Tone Color)
4. Duration	4. Duration

Frequency is the number of complete wave cycles which occur per second. The greater the frequency, the higher the pitch. Amplitude (dynamic level) (or, more commonly, but inaccurately, "volume") is the power or force of the disturbance. The greater the violence of the disturbance, the "louder" will be the tone.

Harmonic constitution (tone color) is a difficult concept. A sound wave is not a simple disturbance. It is filled with imperfections and sub-waves, called "overtones" (or, "upper partials," or "harmonics"). The "fundamental" (first partial, or, first harmonic) is the tone heard, while the upper partials give the tone its quality (color). A tone rich in upper partials, like an oboe, is penetrating and pungent. A sound which lacks upper partials is smooth and pure, like a flute.

Duration is just what it says: how long the disturbance lasts. The acoustician and the musician use the same term here, duration.

Considering the above four qualities of the sound wave, then, any given musical tone may be (1) high or low, (2) loud or soft, (3) penetrating or bland, and (4) long or short. In addition, several other characteristics may be identified in a musical tone.

(5) A musical tone may have vibrato or be without vibrato. Vibrato is the pulsating of a tone caused by pitch changes and by changes in the dynamic level. Appalachian folk singers tend to have a fast narrow vibrato in their sound. Operatic baritones tend to have a slow wide vibrato.

(6) A musical tone may be natural or artificial. In the old days, all tones were "natural," that is, coming from strings, reeds, pipes, skins, and such. Today, through the enormous advances in technology, there are hundreds of varieties of "artificial" sounds coming from synthesizers, ring modulators, and other hardware.

(7) A musical tone may be rendered open or muted. "Mutes" exist for nearly all natural instruments, and these mutes change the tone quality by drastically altering the properties of the sound wave. Until synthesizers came along, brass players had the most options for changing their sound with an assortment of cup mutes, straight mutes, high hats, buckets, broken beer bottles, bathroom plungers, and anything else handy.

(8) Musical tones may be pure or mixed. The infinite combinations of instruments and voices and natural and artificial sounds make music very exciting, these days, and everybody is active. Rock and fusion musicians, classical composers, and all in between are hard at work exploiting the multiple joys of musical tone.

RHYTHM

In her classic *Feeling and Form*, Philosopher Suzanne Langer defines rhythm as "the setting up of new tensions by the resolution of former ones."[2] In music, there are thee aspects to this tension-resolution syndrome: (1) organization, (2) character and speed, and (3) deviations and irregularities.

Organization

The rhythmic drive of a piece of music may arise internally from the needs of the text, or externally from the dictates of a predetermined beat pattern. A beat pattern is called a meter, and the beat-oriented approach thus called metrical music. The text-oriented approach is called, for want of a better term, nonmetrical music. They are not exactly mutually exclusive operations, always, and sometimes there is a touch of each in the other.

Large bodies of music are performed in a text-oriented nonmetrical delivery. Gregorian Chant, the original service music of the Roman Catholic Church, is rendered not according to any preconceived beat pattern, but according to the free ebb and flow of the language of the text. Jewish intoned prayers and cantillations, also. Undulating waves of stresses grow naturally out of the rising and falling nuances of the individual words of the text and out of the syntactical arrangement of the words in the unfolding narrative. The effect is one of profound beauty and expressivity.

This nonmetrical delivery of a text appears in several liturgies (patterns of formal worship): in the more formal Lutheran services, in the Greek Orthodox Church, and in the service music of some other Christian and non-Christian faiths. Nonmetrical delivery of a text is also found outside the area of religious music. Jazz and pop singers will often present the verse of a tune completely free of any beat pattern, then settle into a comfortable pulse for the refrain (chorus).

The whole purpose, and effect, of nonmetrical presentations is to draw attention to the message of the text, while still providing a musical setting of pleasure and comfort. The technique succeeds in doing just that, and its widespread use testifies to its effectiveness in many different musical situations.

By and large, however, most music today comes in organized, beat-oriented, that is, metrical, order. The beat pattern, the meter, is so indicated by a meter signature, consisting of two Arabic numerals, one over the other. The upper numeral indicates "how many" and the bottom numeral "what kind" of notes will be offered in each measure of the music. Thus $\frac{3}{4}$ means "three quarter notes per measure." And $\frac{5}{8}$ means "five eight notes per measure." These meter signatures tell nothing about the speed or character of the music; they merely establish a given base for the notation of the musical ideas.

Music theorists are not in complete agreement about the classification of meter, but the following categories are common.

(1) Simple meter means that there are no extra factors involved. Just straight-forward pulse groups in sets of two counts per measure (called duple meter) (like "Stars and Stripes Forever"), or three counts per measure (triple meter) (like "Happy Birthday), or four counts per measure (quadruple meter) (like "Yesterday").

(2) Compound meter means that there are extra dimensions to the pulse groupings. Sousa's "El Capitan," for example, is in two large beats per measure, but below the surface, there are six subsidiary beats at work. Whereas "Stars and Stripes" goes along with a beat pattern of ONE-TWO, ONE-TWO, ONE-TWO, "El Capitan" goes along with a beat pattern of ONE-two-three FOUR-five-six, ONE-two-three FOUR-five-six. The emphases on ONE and FOUR give a kind of large-scale duple feeling, while a secondary small-scale six-pulse feeling grows out of the ONE-two-three FOUR-five-six delivery. This double layer of rhythmic events is what gives the meter its name, compound meter. "Greensleeves," also, moves along in two layers of activity: two large beats per measure, but below the surface, a ONE-two-three FOUR-five-six subdivision is at work.

In the early days of rock, a kind of fetish developed in the use of $\frac{12}{8}$ meter. Elvis, Fats Domino, Buddy Holly, and all the giants in the business did it time and again. Da-da-da, DA-da-da, DA-da-da, DA-da-da became almost a trademark in early rock. More recently $\frac{12}{8}$ meter served well for Chicago's treatment of "Colour My World."

(3) Complex (asymmetric) meter means that the rhythmic activity might be complicated by the use of unusual groups or arrangements. Three possibilities:

34

(a) The continuous use of an unusual meter, like $\frac{5}{4}$ or $\frac{7}{4}$, through an entire composition. This is called complex (asymmetric) meter (which is also the generic term for the whole technique of using unusual groups or arrangements). A good example is the tune "Everything's Alright" from *Superstar*. This tune is in $\frac{5}{4}$ meter most of the way. So is Paul Desmond's "Take Five," and his later work, "Take Ten" is in $\frac{10}{4}$ meter. Don Ellis has carried unusual meters to astonishing heights. At his peak, he routinely worked in $\frac{19}{4}$, $\frac{11}{8}$, and other complex meters. His "Blues in Elf" is in $\frac{11}{4}$ meter, and "Indian Lady" in $\frac{5}{4}$ meter.

All this is not so new. Tchaikovsky put the second movement of his *Symphony No. 6* in $\frac{5}{4}$ meter, and Stravinsky wrote in unusual meters extensively in the early 1900s. What is new is the wide-spread use of complex meters in jazz and rock.

(b) The sequential use of different meters is called mixed meter. The chorus (refrain) of the Beatles' "Good Day Sunshine" is a splendid example of mixed meter. It has one measure of $\frac{3}{4}$, then four measures of $\frac{4}{4}$, then a final measure of $\frac{5}{4}$ meter. The "Promenade" theme from Mussorsky's *Pictures at an Exhibition* mixes $\frac{6}{4}$ and $\frac{5}{4}$ meters throughout. Neil Diamond's "Song Sung Blue" has one clever little measure of $\frac{2}{4}$ inserted into an otherwise completely $\frac{4}{4}$ tune. Stravinsky and Bartok used mixed meters way back in the 20s and 30s. The technique has finally found its way into pop and jazz and rock and fusion. The effect is, of course, to give the music a new subtle lift by gently breaking the monotony of a strict consistent meter.

(c) Polymeter—the simultaneous use of different meters (by different members of the performing group)—is not very common. To have the violins in $\frac{5}{4}$ and the trombones in $\frac{6}{8}$ and the percussion in $\frac{7}{8}$ is difficult. Rock and fusion groups have been toying around with polymeters recently, with considerable success. Charles Ives (1874-1954), a classical composer, frequently wrote polymetrical things, his *Concord Sonata*, among others.

Character and Speed

In addition to its organization, the rhythmic activity of a given piece of music will show certain qualities of character and speed (*tempo*). For many years, the two factors were suggested by Italian terms like *andante* ("going" or "moving"), *allegro* ("cheerful") and other rather vague terms which permitted some differences of interpretation. Tradition and good musical sense tended to remove the vagueness, though, and internal musical considerations forced themselves upon the performer until something like *allegro* became a fairly predictable designation of style and speed.

From lowest and most solemn to fastest and most energetic, the following terms have come into common use:

Grave	= very slow and somber	Moderato	= moderate
Largo	= broad and very slow	Allegro	= cheerful
Lento	= slow	Vivace	= lively
Adagio	= rather slow	Presto	= quite fast
Andante	= walking along		

Much confusion exists in the diminutive and superlative forms of these terms. Generally speaking, the superlative form means "more so" in the direction of the basic meaning (*larghissimo* = slower and more broad than *largo*; *prestissimo* = faster than *presto*), while the diminutive form means "less so" in the direction of the basic meaning (*larghetto* = less slow and less broad than *largo*; *allegretto* = not quite as cheerful as *allegro*). The problem comes in determining whether the speed ought to be faster than *allegro*, or slower than *allegro*, in order to get *allegretto* (something less cheerful). Even more problematic is *andantino*. Is it faster or slower than *andante*? That is, to create something "less walking," should it go faster or slower than "walking"? Beethoven was confused about all these things, and said so in a letter to his friend and sometime collaborator-publisher, George Thomson. Suffice to say that the general rule of "more so" is the basic idea for the superlative and "less so" of the basic idea for the diminutive seems to provide musicians with a rough guide to interpretation.

Many composers and editors now put a metronome mark at the beginning of the music to specify the exact speed which they feel will give the music its most effective reading. Since its invention by Johann Maelzel in the early 1800s, the metronome has served students and professionals alike in setting consistent and accurate speeds for music. An indication of M.M. (Metronome Marking) = 120 (or, sometimes, ♩ = 120), for example, means that the composer or editor thinks that 120 quarter notes per minute will be a good tempo for the music.

Deviations and Irregularities

Within a given metrical organization, and within a given declaration of character and speed, several techniques for deviating from the expected delivery have become common.

The term *ad libitum* tells the performer to render the music freely, "at will." Vocal music sometimes has *"recitativo,"* that is, in a free recitation-like manner. And the term *rubato* means that the performer should give the passage a good deal of emotional give-and-take, "robbing" a little here and there from a straight-forward rhythmic drive.

Syncopation is the act of putting an accent where it would ordinarily not occur, or removing an accent from where it ordinarily would occur. Syncopation gives a kind of jazzy emphasis to a phrase, but it has become so common, especially in popular music, that it is not always recognized.

The term *cross rhythms* is sometimes used for melodic patterns which are at odds with their underlying rhythmic setting. Glenn Miller's famous treatment of the Andy Razaf and Joe Garland classic "In the Mood," for example, draws its musical interest from the three-note melodic motive lodged in a four eighth-note setting.

MELODY

A succession of tones is called a melody. For all practical purposes, melody is still one of the central threads of the musical experience—in spite of the questionable position of melody, as such, these days, in the modern works of many composers since 1930 or so.

Character

(1) Melody may be conjunct or disjunct. Conjunct melodies have the tones close together. Disjunct melodies have many leaps and skips in time. "White Christmas" is fairly conjunct. "Tie a Yellow Ribbon" is rather disjunct. Many melodies are a little of each, of course.

(2) Melody may be diatonic or chromatic. Diatonic (dia = "through"—thus, through the tones) melodies stay in the key of their origin. The Christmas carol, "Joy to the World," for example. Chromatic (chroma = "color"—thus, color tones) melodies have many deviations, through the use of sharps and flats (called chromatics, or, accidentals). "Flight of the Bumble Bee," for example.

(3) Melody may be tonal, or atonal, or polytonal. Tonal melodies have a point of reference, a kind of "home plate," or base of operation, and they will often end of this home plate tone. "Twinkle, Twinkle, Little Star," for example, opens and closes on this tonal home plate (called the tonic).

Atonal melodies have no such specific center of gravity, although they often work around a kind of arbitrary point of reference. After 1925 or so, many classical composers wrote atonal music with considerable success. Examples of atonal music in folk and jazz and pop fields are extremely rare.

Polytonal melodies work in two or more keys at the same time. The effect is a little startling, and it does just what it is meant to do—throw the whole musical experience into an unpredictable state of affairs in order to avoid the traditional-predictable patterns of anticipation and reward.

(4) A melody may be in a high tessitura or a low tessitura. Tessitura is simply a scholar's term for the general area of activity of the melody. If a baritone singer or a clarinet player is working out of fairly high regions for his voice or instrument, the melody is considered to be in a high tessitura. Beethoven kept the tenors singing in the upper limits of their voices all through the last movement of the Ninth Symphony.

(5) A melody may have a wide or a narrow range, that is, the distance from the lowest to the highest note may be great or small. An occasional high note or low note in a given melody is not as troublesome for a singer as an uncomfortable tessitura.

Length and Function

(6) Melodies may be regular or irregular in phrase length. Melodies in phrase lengths of 4 and 8 measures (or multiples thereof) are considered to be regular. Most of the great pop tunes of the first half of the 20th century have regular eight-measure phrases. The Beatles' "Yesterday" is a nice example of a tune with an opening, irregular, seven-measure phrase. And Buck Owens' version of "I Know You're Married, But I Love You Still" has five-measure phrases throughout the entire composition, including the introduction. Mozart was fond of six-measure phrases, as in, for example, his *Symphony No. 40*, III Movement.

(7) Melody may also be examined in the way it builds up. A good comparison can be made between music and language:

MUSIC	LANGUAGE
(a) note	(a) syllable
(b) motive	(b) word
(c) theme	(c) clause
(d) phrase	(d) sentence
(e) period	(e) paragraph
(f) section	(f) chapter
(g) movement	(g) part or unit
(h) composition	(h) composition

The smallest parcel of musical information is a note. Put a couple of notes together, and it is called a motive. Two or more motives produce a theme. And so on—with the comparison in the way music and language build up length and continuity. All this is arbitrary, imperfect, and only partially true, of course, and any professional musician could argue strongly against the two lists. Debatable as this comparison is, it still provides a useful generalized idea of the way melody accrues length.

(8) Melodies often come in a verse-and-refrain design. The verse-and-refrain principle is nearly universal in all forms and styles of music. The verse describes the situation of love, or unhappiness, or whatever; the refrain suspends the narrative, temporarily, to offer an artistic statement on the general emotional state of affairs. Thousands of folk ballads demonstrate the effectiveness of this principle.

The recitative-and-aria design in opera derives from the same principle. The recitative describes the narrative circumstances; the aria freezes the situation, temporarily, to offer an artistic statement on that fixed condition.

In popular and folk music, the terms refrain and chorus are interchangeable. In operas and oratorios, the term aria means that a single vocalist will do the job, while the term chorus means that a group of singers will deliver the "refrain."

This comparison of verse-and-refrain and recitative-and-aria principles is imperfect and only partially true (as was the comparison between music and language, above), but, again, it provides a general notion as to the way certain basic psycho-emotional urges are manifest in various musical subcultures. Things may happen one way in country music ballads, and another way in grand opera, but both audiences are responding to the same basic human desire for musico-dramatic gratification.

(9) A melody, or portions of a melody, may come to a cadence frequently, or things may spin out for a long time without a cadence. A cadence (from *cadire* = "to fall") is that moment when the melody pauses, gathers its breath, so to speak, and strikes out on another musical mission. Brahms was so clever at concealing his cadences that his music seems to spin on in unduly long gestures. Wagner took great pains to actually avoid any real cadential pauses. The Beatles were fond of bringing their melodies to a cadence slightly before the chords and rhythm came to that cadence. In country music, the cadences are often prolonged and savored.

HARMONY

The simultaneous sounding of several different pitches is called harmony. For well over 300 years, harmony was central to Western music. It has lost its great position today, however, in the music of Varese, Boulez, Ussachevsky, and other modernists, although it is still very much a part of the thinking of Menotti, Aaron Copland, and many others.

(1) Harmony may be tertian or non-tertian. Tertian harmony gets its name from the fact that it derives from a piling up of notes which are 3 tones distant. C-E-G on the piano, for

example. Non-tertian harmony is based on a different piling up of vertical sounds—in fourths, or fifths, or some other pre-arranged clusters.

(2) Harmony may be tonal, atonal, or polytonal. As with melody, the term "tonal" means fixed with a center of gravity, a kind of home plate. This condition may arise from a setting in (a) the traditional major or minor scales, or (b) one of the several "modes," "The Christmas Song" ("Chestnuts roasting on an open fire..."), for example opens with an octave leap then a descending line which derives from the tonal/major scale harmony of the tune. "O Come, O Come, Immanuel" is, however, in tonal/modal harmony.

Atonal harmony usually grows out of 12-tone (serial, or dodecaphonic) musical procedures. Serial composers set up an arbitrary string (series) of the 12 different available tones which serves as the basic "scale" material for the piece of music. Dodecaphonic (dodeca = 12) compositions have a kind of "harmony," then, chosen from clusters of tones which the composer has selected for the work. Each new 12-tone composition is a law unto itself, complete with a new "scale" (series of tones) as the raw material of its art.

Polytonal harmony means that two or more keys are used at the same time. To get the effect, think of "Happy Birthday" played at the piano in the key of B in the left hand, and the key of A in the right hand, with a guitarist accompanying all this in the key of F—and everything happening at the same time. it is not as bad as it first sounds, as Stravinsky, Prokofiev, Milhaud, Ives, and others demonstrated so well in some passages of their music.

(3) Harmony may be consonant or dissonant. The terms are strictly relative, for what is now consonant may have been quite dissonant for earlier ears. Generally speaking, consonant harmony means "pleasing." The question is, "Pleasing to whom? When?" Debussy's music, for example, is quite pleasing today, but it was quite displeasing to his professors at the Paris Conservatory in the late 1800s. And what is pleasing to Miles Davis might have been quite displeasing to Louis Armstrong. Still, in spite of their relative nature, the terms are useful in describing one aspect of harmony.

(4) Harmony may be functional or non-functional. Functional harmony proceeds in traditional root movements, and the chords seem to proceed comfortably (to Western ears) along predictable paths. Non-functional harmony simply supports things without regard for the predictable paths. The parallel-coloristic harmonies of Debussy and Ravel are frequently non-functional in this sense.

(5) Harmony may be progressive or retrogressive. Progressive harmony seems to move the music along in a sense of forward motion. This is, of course, a conditioned response, peculiar to Western Culture, and it is highly unlikely that going from C-seventh to F-seventh to B-flat feels the same to an Australian native as it does to Buck Owens or Van Cliburn. John Denver's "Country Roads" proceeds (or recedes) along what might be called a path of retrogressive harmony, for the chords move from G, to E-minor, to D, to C, and finally back to G. This is not at all the way "Sweet Georgia Brown" went back in the 1930s: D-seventh, to G-seventh, to C-seventh, to the tonic, F chord, for the opening few phrases.

(6) Several miscellaneous terms are handy to know. Jazz musicians use the term *changes* and the term *progressions* to refer to the chords which are proper for a given tune.

As with melody, the term cadence refers to a moment in the unfolding of the music when there seems to be a kind of "point of arrival," and the music comes to a breathing spot, as it were, to gather itself up before striking out on a new assignment. Cadences in the melody and harmony and rhythm usually occur at the same time, although they need not.

Modulation is the act of moving from one key to another. The event may take place in a long, carefully prepared, operation, as in Mozart's modulation from the key of G-minor to B-flat major to get from the first theme to the second theme in his *Symphony No. 40*, Movement I. A modulation may also take place with a few swift strokes, as in the last few measures of "Killing Me Softly With His Song."

TEXTURE
Texture is the most difficult of all the common components of music of understand, partly because of the

difficulty of the concept itself, and partly because the term is often used for something else. The term is often used to describe the feel-taste of a given orchestral passage of music, almost like "texture" of ice cream, only in ear-oriented rather than tongue-oriented sensations. In the traditional musical sense, however, the term texture refers to the relationship between horizontal (melodic lines) and vertical (chords) gestures in music.

(1) Monophonic texture refers to the condition of only one event—one line, or one "voice," as it is called—doing all the work. No chords. No counter-melodies. No percussion instruments. Just a single melodic thread carrying the entire musical experience.

(2) Polyphonic texture refers to the condition of many voices (individual "lines" whether rendered by singers or by instrumentalists) contributing to the total musical fabric. Each musical voice has a kind of independent melodic mission of its own. Sometimes these independent voices imitate each other very closely, as in a contrapuntal (from counterpoint, "point against point") work by Bach or Handel. Sometimes the voices carry out distinct little missions of their own which do not imitate, but, rather, complement each of the other voices, as in a Dixieland arrangement, for example, with the trumpet on the melody, the clarinet on ornamental lacework, and the trombone on a kind of countermelody in the basement.

(3) Homophonic texture refers to the condition of a top voice delivering the major musical message, while the lower voices support things in a subservient role. Most pop, folk, rock, jazz, and country music is in homophonic texture. Most classical music from Mozart to the present is, likewise, in homophonic texture.

(4) Heterophonic texture refers to the condition of several performers (voices or instruments) offering slightly modified versions of the same melody. Heterophonic texture is nearly non-existent in Western classical music, but it is a big part of the music of Chinese, Japanese, African, and other cultures. It is also a big part of jazz, especially at jam sessions where there are several like instruments in the group, each playing the basic melody in an individualistic free manner.

(5) Electronophonic texture might be a term coined for all the exciting sounds of the modernists, both in classical music and in jazz and rock. The old ideas about melodic lines, "voices," supporting harmonies, and such traditional concepts are meaningless here, of course, for the pure sensations of the sounds, themselves, have become a major factor in the musical experience offered by Stockhausen, and Xenakis, and Pink Floyd, and sometimes Miles Davis.

EXPRESSIVE DEVICES

The sixth component of music which is common to all forms and styles in Western Culture is a whole battery or tricks which might be called expressive devices. Music is seldom offered in a pure state; it is nearly always charged with emotional additions.

(1) *Accelerando* (getting faster) and *ritardando* (getting slower) give a musical passage greater potency by kicking in new energy (accelerando), or by pulling things to a majestic conclusion (ritardando). Pop singers frequently draw out the end of their tunes with a ritard. So did Handel and Bach and Vivaldi and Torelli. In his Fifth Symphony, however, Beethoven achieved the desired sense of finality by a sudden accelerando into the closing moments, and then hammered home the final chords with all his characteristic aggressive power.

(2) *Forte* (loud) and *piano* (soft)—"dynamic levels," as they are called—are central to musical expressivity, rock concerts notwithstanding. Loud and soft passages of music may be gradually developed (*crescendo* = getting louder; *decrescendo*, or, *diminuendo* = getting softer). Or, loud and soft moments may come quickly, without preparation (*sforzato* = suddenly very loud; *subto piano* = suddenly very soft).

(3) Techniques of *staccato* (separated) and *legato* (connected) give certain musical passages the appropriate emotional thrust. The opening motive of Beethoven's Fifth Symphony simply would not make sense any other way than separated (they are not actually marked with staccato dots but are traditionally rendered quite distinct and clear); and Kris Kristofferson's "Help Me Make It Through The Night" would

not be quite the same if it were sung in a crisp staccato manner.

(4) *Portamento* (sliding from one note to another) is absolutely essential for opera singers, although not as essential as some are inclined to make it. Pop singers, too; and certainly for country steel-guitar players. This continuous-thread delivery makes the music much more comfortable than would abrupt changes from one note to another.

(5) The *trill* (a rapid alternation of a given note with its upper neighbor) often occurs on the penultimate (next to the last) note of a phrase, and draws the listener to the concluding note with a feeling of satisfying finality. It works every time.

(6) *Mordents* are standard operating procedure for musicians. The upper mordent (a note, then its upper neighbor, then the original note again) became a trademark in Bing Crosby's singing. Nancy Wilson and Miles Davis have used the lower mordent (a note, then its lower neighbor, then the original note again) with great finese for many years.

Dozens more of these expressive devices are found in all styles and varieties of music. In classical music, there are turns, appoggiaturas, anticipations, grace notes, and other embellishments (also called ornaments). In jazz, there are drops, and smears, and growls, and screams. In country music, there is that insistent pain-filled nasal twang, and that peculiar thing called yodeling. In rock, there are feedback gimmicks, fuzz tones, reverberation tricks, and a whole battery of electronic marvels.

All in all, the diverse stock of expressive devices as practiced by musicians of all ilk and hue give the art of music enormously increased emotional territory. Without these expressive devices, things would be dull, indeed.

READING NOTES FOR CHAPTER FIVE

[1]Hughson Mooney, "Popular Music Before Ragtime, 1840-1890: Some Implications for the Study of American Culture," in *Popular Music and Society*, Volume V (1977), No. 5, pp. 17-18.

[2]Susanne K. Langer, *Feeling and Form* (New York: Charles Scribner's Sons, 1953), p. 127.

Principles of Single-Unit
Musical Form

All musical operations, from simple folk ballads to elaborate symphonies, obey certain laws of organization and form. To be satisfying at all, every musical composition must have a generous measure of unity to keep it glued together as an experience, and a touch of variety to give it some subsidiary areas of interest. The whole art of musical composition might be summarized as a composer's struggle to present the right amount of unity and variety. The "right amount" differs, of course, with the announced intent of the musical work, but the problem is essentially the same whether it is "A Symphonic Poem on Universal Love" or the "Wabash Cannonball."

From the simplest to the most complex, the following principles of form are found in the music of Western Civilization.

ILLUSTRATION: A raked opera stage under construction. Courtesy of the CCM Publicity Office, Cincinnati, Ohio.

ONE-PART FORM

"You Are My Sunshine" serves well to get started: sixteen measures of music; two phrases, eight measures each; very few deviations or complications. "Amazin' Grace," also: sixteen measures of music; two phrases, eight measures each; very few elaborations. Chopin's "Prelude No. 7, Opus 28," also: sixteen measures of music; two phrases, eight measures each; very few deviations from the original opening melodic lines.

BINARY FORM

Two kinds of binary form are found in music. Scholars show the design scheme of these forms, and other musical forms, with a system of letters and numbers.

The A-B Design

"America" is a good example of the A-B kind of two-part form: two little sections, one complementing the other.

A My country, 'tis of thee, sweet land of liberty,
Of thee I sing.

B Land where my father's died, land of the pilgrims' pride,
From every mountain side, let freedom ring.

"Greensleeves" turns out to be in two little sections, also, each section consisting of a distinct musical contour.

A Alas, my love, you do me wrong to cast me off discourteously.
And I have loved you, oh, so long, delighting in your company.

B Greensleeves was all my joy; Greensleeves was my delight.
Greensleeves was my heart of gold, and who, but my lady Greensleeves.

The A-A' Design

A slightly different kind of binary form is often found. It might be diagrammed as A-A' (A and A-prime): two sections of music, the second being nearly identical to the first, except for a change at the end to tie things up in a satisfying manner. "Stardust," "Pennies from Heaven," and "Put on a Happy Face" are good examples. So is Henry Mancini's "Moon River." And Jerry Herman's "Hello, Dolly!"

TERNARY FORM

One of the most common forms in all of music. It satisfies a deep human need for the return of familiar melodic material.

The A-B-A Design

"Twinkle, Twinkle, Little Star" certainly demonstrates the principle.

A Twinkle, twinkle, little star,
   How I wonder what you are.
B Up above the clouds so high,
   Like a diamond in the sky.
A Twinkle, twinkle, little star,
   How I wonder what you are.

The A-A-B-A Design

Often, a psychological need is felt to repeat the first little section of music, to fix it firmly in mind, before the contrasting center section is offered. Thousands of popular songs appear in this design. The Beatles' famous "Yesterday" is an interesting example of this form, because the first two "A" sections are only 7 measures each, rather than the conventional 8 measures in length.

RONDO FORM

The principle of alternating familiar with contrasting sections of music is known as rondo forms. In its simplest design, it might be diagrammed A-B-A-B-A. Dozens of varieties are possible. The second movement of Beethoven's *Piano Sonata in C-minor, Op.* 13, the "Pathetique," for example, is often diagrammed A-B-A-C-A-coda (the *coda* being a little concluding section; coda = Italian for "tail"). The third movement of the same Beethoven piano sonata is a different version of the rondo principle, A-B-A-C-A-B-A-coda.

Whatever may be the character of the contrasting sections (the B and C and other sections), the basic idea (the A section) will keep coming back in a way which is usually not too hard to detect. It is this "return" which gives the rondo its name (rondeau = small circle).

Rondo forms are very common in classical music, especially in the Classical Period (1750-1820), but not very common in popular music at all, although the theme from TV's *Happy Days* has a kind of rondo-like return to a familiar section quite often.

PIANO RAGS AND MILITARY MARCHES

A common musical form which has the vague feeling of a combined binary, ternary, and rondo appeared in the late 1800s, the ragtime piano works of Scott Joplin and others. The form derives from the sectional design of European military marches:

    *   Introduction
    A First Strain (repeated)
    B Second Strain (repeated)
    C Trio
    D Interlude—the "Dog Fight"
    C Trio (in a grandiose manner)

The military march form as sketched out above turns out to be a kind of large scale binary form, the first and second strains being part one and the trio part two. This form was common property when John Phillip Sousa and many others before and after him made the form so familiar to American audiences. The piano rags are build up in 16-measure sections, just like marches.

    *   Introduction
    A First Section (repeated)
    B Second Section (repeated)
    A First Section (not repeated)
    C Third Section (repeated)
    D Fourth Section (repeated)

This form turns out to be a kind of large scale binary form, too. In both forms, above, the third section, Section C, nearly always goes to the key of 4th step of the scale, the subdominant, as it is called.

THEME AND VARIATIONS

Just what it says. A composer presents a basic, fairly simple, unit of music, and then offers several treatments, "variations," of the basic unit. The variations may be mere decorations of the fundamental notes of the original unit of music, or they may be rather severe modifications of the original unit of music. The variations, thus, may be quite obvious, or quite heavily disguised.

Besides the term theme and variations, itself, two other terms are used for works based on this principle: *chaconne* and *passacaglia*. Scholars have been arguing for years about the distinction between the two forms. Suffice to say that chaconne and passacaglia are terms used for works built around a short theme (often only 4 or 8 measures). The theme is not a melody, really, but a succession of chords, often with a bass line (*ostinato*, from Latin *obstinare* = to persist) which gets repeated throughout the bulk of the composition. The ostinato (called, also, the *ground*, or the *ground bass*, or the *basso ostinato*) with its chords above is the foundation for the whole musical operation.

Jazz musicians actually practice this chaconne-passacaglia idea every time they take off on their flights of improvisation. After the original "chart" (chart = a standard tune, or a special arrangement of a standard tune) is delivered by the collective jazz group, each individual musician in the group then offers his personal reflections over the chain of chords of the basic chart. The result is, in every sense, chaconne-passacaglia kind of music making.

One such musical undertaking, a pattern of chords called the blues, is so common and so satisfying that it deserves a special discussion of its own.

THE BLUES

The Blues is a term used to denote an early historical period in the field of jazz (Bessie Smith, and before), and it is a term also used to denote a special kind of down-home style of singing-performing, the kind of authenticity suggested, a few years ago, by the wide use of the term Soul.

As a musical form (that is, a set of chords), the blues is a rigorous contract for the I chord, the IV chord, and the V[7] chord in the following scheme (in the key of C):

C Chord	F Chord	C Chord
(Measures 1 through 4)	(Measures 5 and 6)	(Measures 7 and 8)

G⁷ Chord	C Chord
(Measures 9 and 10)	(Measures 11 and 12)

Scholars and theorists use the Roman numerals when analyzing classical music. Jazz and pop musicians nearly always use names of the specific chords.

At least two other versions of the above classic theoretical blues pattern are found throughout the history of popular music:

C Chord	F Chord	C Chord	C⁷ Chord
(Measure 1)	(Measure 2)	(Measure 3)	Measure 4)

F Chord	C Chord	G⁷ Chord
(Measures 5 and 6)	(Measures 7 and 8)	(Measure 9)

F Chord	C Chord
(Measure 10)	(Measures 11 and 12)

The above pattern appears with seventh and ninth chords generously offered on any or all of the chords as listed. Something similar to the above design serves well for thousands of basic rock 'n' roll tunes. The next pattern, a bit more elaborate, with a nice "drive to the final cadence," has become a favorite in jazz:

C Chord	F Chord	C Chord	C⁷ Chord
(Measure 1)	(Measure 2)	(Measure 3)	(Measure 4)

F Chord	Fmi Chord	C Chord	A⁷ Chord
(Measure 5)	(Measure 6)	(Measure 7)	(Measure 8)

Dmi Chord	G⁷ Chord	C Chord
(Measure 9)	(Measure 10)	(Measures 11 and 12)

The blues pattern, so universally appealing, shows no signs at all of wearing out. Drawn, essentially, from three basic chords (called the primarily triads), the blues pattern permits all melodic gestures because the three chords contain every note in the standard diatonic scale.

BIG BAND AND COMBO CHARTS

Closely related to the blues and ragtime forms are the arrangements of the big bands and combos. These "charts," as the jazz musicians call them, may be completely written out or completely oral, or somewhere between. The bigger the band, the more likely that the arrangement will be largely written out, of course. A typical big band arrangement:[1]

* Introduction
A The Basic Tune (saxophones and brasses alternately have the melody and support materials) or perhaps part of the tune
B Interlude (key change, often)
A The Basic Tune (vocal solo, or instrumental solo)
C Interlude (key change, often)
A The Basic Tune (last half of the tune, perhaps, with some considerable flourish at the end)

The above form is a gross oversimplification of a complex and continually changing condition. In actual practice, in a given arrangement, a spot may be opened up for extended solos by several instrumentalists, after which the leader signals for a return to some final treatment of the basic tune. The possibilities go on forever, but the basic principle of much contrast in and around 2½ to 3 times through a basic tune still obtains for many of the arrangements in the literature of the big bands.

Combo (short for "combination," that is, a group smaller and less rigorously prescribed) arrangements encourage more individualistic offerings, to be sure:

* Introduction
A The Chart (the basic tune or "riff"—a riff being a short memorable motive)
B ⎫
C ⎪
D ⎬ Improvised Solos
E ⎪
F ⎭
G Fours (soloists alternating sections of four measures each, to build a collaborative solo)
H The Chart (sometimes slightly modified, with a tag ending, perhaps)

This, too, is a gross oversimplification of things.[2] Still, the principle of basic material followed by many solos concluded by basic material can be found in thousands of small band recordings and live performances. The technique of "trading fours" came in, new, after World War II, but otherwise the small band manner of delivering a given musical experience has remained constant for the better part of the 20th century. One exception: the very early jazz groups—the Original Dixieland Jazz Band, for example—often had everybody playing all the time. By the late 1920s, though, small band offerings had begun to settle into a fairly predictable formula.

SONATA-ALLEGRO DESIGN

One of the most important of all musical forms. It grows out of the binary dance forms of the Renaissance, but by the time it crystallizes in the Classic Period (1750-1820), sonata-allegro design is, for all practical purposes, a kind of ternary form, best diagrammed as A-B-A.

Sonata-allegro design (also called sonata form, or sonata-allegro form, or first movement form) consists of 3 main sections, the first of which is occasionally repeated in full:

A Exposition
      Theme 1
      Theme 2

B Development
      One or both themes are "worked over,"
      fragments isolated and altered, notes changed,
      bits of the themes put in different keys, etc.

A Recapitulation
      Theme 1 (as above)
      Theme 2 (in a different key)

This basic scheme may be preceded by an introduction; the individual sections will be laced together with connective material called transitions; and the whole form may be concluded with a *coda*. The 3 main sections are the heart of the operation, though, in an A-B-A setting. Surely it is not just a coincidence that this ternary formula is also the most prevalent of the popular song forms, all the way from "Body and Soul" back in the 1930s right up to "Yesterday" from the 1960s. There seems to be something very satisfying about this kind of organizational scheme for the Western mind.

A sonatina is a small-scale version of the above design—with the development section absent, or greatly reduced.

CONTRAPUNTAL FORMS

Contrapuntal forms are forms in which the individual lines ("voices") work with and against each other to produce the total musical package.

The strictest contrapuntal design is the canon (Greek, for "law," or "rule"), in which the same melody appears in the various voices in strict imitation. Like "Row, Row, Row Your Boat" and "Are You Sleeping, Brother John," called rounds, these days, and called *rotas*, in earlier days.

Less strict, but more complex, is the fugue (from Latin *fuga* = flight), with its three ingredients: (a) sets of entries, consisting of the subject and its exact imitations (called real answers) and its slightly altered imitations (called tonal answers) coming in and out of the piece at various times, and (b) episodes (connective material and supportive lines). Bach's three-voice *Fugue in C-minor* is a good example.

The first set of entries in a fugue is often called the exposition. It would seem to be convenient, however, to make a distinction between the opening material in sonata-allegro design (exposition) and the opening material in a fugue by calling the latter a "first set of entries."

MUTATIONAL FORM

In the form known as a symphonic poem, the original musical materials go through rather drastic changes—changes more substantive than the kind of changes found in a theme-and-variations form or in the development section of sonata-allegro design. This mutation of the original melodic material is sometimes called thematic transformation, or thematic metamorphosis. Berlioz, Liszt, Wagner, Sibelius, and other composers used mutational techniques with great success during the late Romantic Period.

A famous case of musical mutation is Berlioz's *Symphonie Fantastique* during which the dominant melodic idea (called, sometimes, the fixed idea) goes through many transformations in the course of the five movements of the symphony. Each change in the melody derives from a change in the character of the girl represented by the melody.

THROUGH-COMPOSED FORMS

Two possibilities: (a) the text, or (b) the original musical gestures, will dictate the organic unfolding of the musico-architectural design, and the composer tries to avoid repetition at all costs.

Through-composed technique (German = *durchkomponiert*) emerged in the Romantic Period, especially in the art songs of Schubert and others. Schubert's *Erlkoenig* is probably one of the world's most famous examples.

Varese and other 20th Century composers have done essentially the same thing in pure musical sounds. The total musical experience grows out of continuously explored-unfolding sounds, with precious little imitation or repetition as design factors. Varese's famous *Electronic Poem* is a splendid example.

READING NOTES FOR CHAPTER SIX

[1]Two typical examples of a big band arrangement are given in Charles Hamm, *Yesterdays: Popular Song in America* (New York: W. W. Norton & Co., 1979), p. 385. In this case, vocal solos are a part of the arrangements.

[2]An excellent discussion of combo charts and improvisation procedures is found in Jerry Coker, *Listening to Jazz* (Englewood Cliffs, New Jersey: Prentice-Hall, Inc., 1978), Chapter 5, "The Improvisers' Hall of Fame," pp. 73-134.

Principles Of Multi-Unit
Musical Form

Chapter Six, "Principles of Single-Unit Musical Form", treated musical form as one continuous, uninterrupted package, that is, in a single-unit statement. This chapter will explain how music is organized on a large scale, in multi-unit (or, composite, or aggregate, or multi-movement) form.

Four basic principles obtain: (a) the collection principle, (b) the pattern principle, and (c) the narrative-thread principle, (d) the emotional syndrome principle.

The Collection Principle

The easiest and most obvious way to put together a large package of music is simply to string together a series of short selections. This is exactly what has happened over and over again throughout the history of music. The result is not boring or simplistic at all. The contrasts between and among the various short works gives the large form its interest and appeal.

ILLUSTRATION: Herbie Hancock and Chick Corea. Courtesy of CBS Records.

In their appropriate places throughout the following pages, many "collection" forms will be discussed.

(a) the suite
(b) the sonata (before 1750)
(c) the concerto (before 1750)
(d) the overture (before 1750)
(e) the song cycle
(f) the concept album
(g) miscellaneous theater pieces—revues, follies, scandals, vanities, and the like
(h) the "set" in the field of popular entertainment, usually a group of tunes lasting around 45 minutes.

The Pattern Principle

Sometimes a grand pattern appears over and over again in the works of many composers of several historical periods. Like a baseball game, each time it happens it is exactly the same—nine players on each team, nine innings, three outs per inning, and so on—yet each time it happens that the individual players do something unique and different from what they did the last game. Likewise with music. Each time is special.

(a) the sonata forms-at-large, with four major sections
(b) the Mass, with its five major sections
(c) the minstrel show, with two large sections
(d) the contemporary TV shows of superstar popular musicians, Lionel Richie, Barbara Mandrell, Kenny Rogers and others

The Narrative Thread Principle

Often a long musical work derives from a story being told in musical language.

(1) Concert Setting
    (a) the oratorio (verbal and specific)
    (b) the cantata (verbal and specific)
    (c) the symphonic poem (non-verbal and free in association)
(2) Stage Setting
    (a) opera and music drama
    (b) operetta and Broadway musicals

The Emotional Syndrome Principle

Modern composers and performers sometimes launch into a delivery of musical gestures with no prescribed scheme in mind, knowing that this kind of free flow of musical consciousness can often produce artistic results. The extended improvisatory excursions by jazz musicians Keith Jarrett, Bob James, Chick Corea, and others hearken back to John Coltrane's "sheets of sound." Ornette Coleman's "free form jazz" derives largely from purposefully unprepared musical plan. Likewise the free flights of rhapsodic fancy offered by rock virtuosos Jimi Hendrix, Keith Emerson, and Eric Clapton when they were in their prime.

In classical music, the same kind of effort toward spontaneous creativity, called the principle of indeterminacy, motivated John Cage (b. 1912) in his *Imaginary Landscape* (1951) for 12 radios, 24 "players," and one conductor, and in his *4 Minutes and 33 Seconds* (1954), in three movements, during which the pianist sits silent before the piano for the entire duration of the work.

Karlheinz Stockhausen (b. 1928) has searched elsewhere for unpredictable musical experiences. His *Cycle for Percussion* (1959) puts a lone percussionist inside a circle of instruments to play at will for a specified time, starting wherever is convenient and working around in a clockwise or counter-clockwise movement until returning to the initial instruments. Stockhousen and Cage are pursuing the art of aleatoric (chance) music in the works mentioned above.

Lukas Foss (b. 1922) has tried to introduce the art of improvisation into classical music. The old masters—Bach, Handel, Mozart, Beethoven—improvised often and well, but later composers gradually removed the possibility by prescribing everything for the performer. In *Time Cycle* (1960), Foss permits improvisatory interludes between the written sections of the music.

Edgard Varese's (1883-1965) *Electronic Poem* created a different emotional landscape for each of the listeners who heard it as they walked through the enormous kidney-shaped pavilion at the Brussels World's Fair in 1958. Over 400 speakers produced a radial acoustic experience which cannot possibly be demonstrated or duplicated.

Contemporary *minimalist* composers create an emotional syndrome with precisely the opposite technique. Rather than chance sounds, minimalists present simple musical fragments repeated with maddening regularity until a kind of hypnotic trance-like emotional stasis set in—thereby opening the listener to whatever unpredictable feelings might arise.

By various techniques, then, modern musicians are trying to offer a broad musical experience without the conventional formal procedures of collection, pattern, or narrative—but, rather, by the principle of creating an emotional syndrome.

Part III
Instruments and Instrumental Forms

8

Instruments and Instrumental Combinations

Since the beginning of history, humankind has been driven to get together singly and in groups to blow, thump, and scrape away on musical instruments. The following ingenius categorization by the German historian, Curt Sachs, covers all the instruments in existence.

SCIENTIFIC CATEGORIES
Idiophones

If the sound is produced by the instrument, itself, the instrument is called an *idiophone* (Greek *idios* = self). Several sub-categories exist.

(1) Struck. Xylophones, gongs, bells, castanets, cymbals, triangles, chimes, wood blocks, many Oriential instruments, etc.

(2) Shaken. Rattles, maracas, tambourines, etc.

(3) Plucked. Jew's harps (not juice harps, notice), music boxes, etc.

(4) Rubbed. Glass harmonicas, musical saws, etc.

Membranophones

If the sound is produced by some kind of elastic material stretched over a resonating chamber, the instrument is called a *membranophone* (Latin *membranum* = skin). Like snare drums, bass drums, timpani (kettle drums), etc.

Aerophones

If the sound is produced by an activated column of air, the instrument is called an *aerophone* (Green *aeros* = air, wind). Several sub-categories.

(1) Free Aerophones. A free reed driven by forced air. Accordions, concertinas, harmoniums (the little organs played by the members of the Salvation Army at Christmas time), etc.

(2) Wind Instruments. An enclosed column of air.
(a) Brass Instruments. Trumpets, horns, trombones, cornets, etc., in which the player's compressed lips generate the disturbance which causes the air column to vibrate.

(b) Flutes. Dozens of varieties of vertical flutes (Coke-bottle style), cross flutes, and whistles, etc., in which an air stream is split, setting it into vibration.

(c) Reed Pipes. Both single reed instruments (clarinets, saxophones) and double reed instruments (oboes, bassoons) in which a fixed reed sets the air column into motion.

Chordophones

If the sound is produced by a string under tension, the instrument is called a *chordophone* (Greek *choros* = string). By far, the largest and most diverse category of instruments commonly used.

(1) The Zither Family. The strings are parallel to the reconating body or stick. Pianos, harpsichords, dulcimers, clavichords, zithers, autoharps, etc., and the steel guitar.

(2) The Lute Family. The strings are parallel to the resonating body only part way, and the remainder of the strings are streteched out over and along a neck. Violins, guitars, banjos, lutes, etc.

(3) The Lyre Family. The strings are connected to a crossbar between two sides of a yoke. Lyres, kitharas, etc.

(4) The Harp Family. The strings are vertical to the sound resonating chamber. The harp is the only instrument of this kind in Occidental culture.

Electronophones

To Curt Sachs' original classification, a modern extension should be made for instruments which produce sounds, or greatly alter existing sounds, through electronic means. Synthesizers, ring modulators, tone generators, and other ingenious gadgets are a standard part of the art of music today.

COMMON STRING-DOMINATED ENSEMBLES

String-Dominated Combinations

The Symphony Orchestra

There are three large sections in a typical symphony orchestra: (1) the strings, (2) the winds, and (3) the percussion. Everyone in each section plays from a highly detailed printed page, and delivers the notes on cue. Except for some recent modern works, there is no room for "making up" or improvising in the orchestra. The conductor of the orchestra has a full score on which every separate note for each player is indicated.

The strings—violins, violas, cellos, and basses—carry the burden of the musical chores, usually, and the winds and percussion will color, punctuate, reinforce, and embellish the musical offering. The work-horse string section is on duty about 80 percent of the time; the winds about 40 percent; and the percussion about 20 percent.

The relative proportion of strings against winds and percussion is surprisingly consistent from the very small orchestra in the days of Mozart and Haydn (the Classic Period, 1750-1820) to the days of Brahms and Mahler (the Romantic Period, 1820-1900). The distribution is roughly 2/3 strings and 1/3 winds and percussion. An orchestra in the Classic Period, for example, might have perhaps 20 strings, and 8-10 winds, with, occasionally, a timpani player, for a total of somewhere around 28-32 players.

With Brahms and other late Romantics, the orchestra grew to gigantic dimensions, anywhere from 90 to 120 players, but the distribution was still roughly 2/3 strings and 1/3 winds and percussion. A Mahler symphony, for example, might call for 60 or more strings, with 35-40 winds and percussion. Generally speaking, the strings grew in numbers only, while the winds and percussion grew in numbers and in exotic varieties— contrabassoons, harps, pianos, wind machines, special tubas, also flutes, chimes, bass trombones, xylophones, wood blocks, gongs, rattles, and such.

The String Orchestra

Just what it says. Strings only—violins, violas, cellos, and double-basses. Less capable of musical fireworks than the full symphony orchestra, obviously, and thus inclined toward musical introversion and reflection. Music for string orchestra will not rely on coloristic diversity as much as it will on pure musical substance (melody, harmony, rhythm, etc.).

Chamber String Groups

(a) Duets of two violins, or of violin and viola, or of violin and cello, or of viola and cello, etc., sometimes with piano accompaniment, sometimes without piano accompaniment, are common, especially in classical music.

(b) The most common string trio is violin, viola, and cello. Other combinations are around, but not as often.

(c) Far and away, the most important chamber string group is the string quartet. Almost every major classical composer from Mozart on took a shot at string quartet music. It is extremely fulfilling and satisfying in every way, but extremely difficult to serve well. With only four instruments—2 violins, a viola, and a cello—there can be no wasted effort, no throw-away gestues. Music, pure music, and nothing but the music, here. Beethoven's string quartets are considered among the highest forms.

(d) Quintets, sextets, septets, octets, etc., are around, too. No specific line of demarcation exists, but after 8 or 9 instruments, the piece is likely to lose the number-designating title, and be called simply a piece for a small string ensemble.

(e) A special kind of chamber string combination is the appearance of the piano with any of the above. The name then becomes piano trio (piano, violin, cello), or piano quartet (piano, violin, viola, cello), or piano quintet (piano, 2 violins, viola, cello) and so on.

Country and Western Groups

The classic Blue Grass band used to be fiddle, guitar, banjo, mandolin, and string bass. More and more, the "New Grass" groups are adding drums and a steel guitar. The essential sound of country music, though, is a string sound, and the tradition goes all the way back to dulcimers, fiddles, banjos, guitars, and string basses—unamplified then, but everything amplified, now, among the mainstream commercial stars.

Rock Groups

A great number of rock groups were, and are, string dominated. The Beatles' core instrumentation was three guitars (rhythmn, lead, and bass) and drums. Dozens of both American and British groups made dozens of hits without piano or horns as really significant elements in the concept.

COMMON HORN-DOMINATED ENSEMBLES
The Military Band

Throughout all of recorded history, military bands have inspired soldiers to great victories. Modern high school and college bands follow that tradition with a generous measure of pageantry and power for America's sporting events.

After marching season, the American bands move indoors to become the schools' concert bands, and a curious kind of transformation begins to throw the clarinet section into a role similar to the string section in the orchestra. Not so many clarinets (one-third clarinets to two-thirds other winds in the band, perhaps), but the clarinets become the work-horse section quite often in a good number of band compositions.

Many American and European variations on the "military band" model exist, to be sure. The British have all brass bands, no reed instruments, and the sound is a rich organ-like texture of surprising warmth and beauty.

Drum and Bugle Corps, Shrine Bands, even bagpipe groups, and others, each with a special sound and style, all share the tradition of providing music of noble stature for ceremonial occasions.

Chamber Wind Groups

(a) As with chamber string groups, various duets have been written for almost any conceivable pairing of wind instruments, with a general tendency to pair woodwinds with woodwinds, and brasses with brasses.

(b) Likewise with wind trios. Typical combinations might be flute, oboe, and clarinet. Or clarinet, oboe, and bassoon. Concert bands will often feature a razzle-dazzle trumpet trio as a special number to brighten up a concert.

(c) Likewise with quartets. Woodwind quartets (flute, oboe, clarinet, bassoon) and brass quartets (trumpet, horn, trombone, tuba; or 2 trumpets, horn, and trombone) appear in classical music with some regularity.

(d) With quintets, two wind groups have become rather standard: (1) The woodwind quintet (flute, clarinet, oboe, French horn, and bassoon) is a favorite. The French horn, being very flexible in tone, has been found over the years to compliment and complement the woodwinds nicely, and is thus a standard item in the woodwind quintet. (2) The Brass quintet (2 trumpets, French horn, trombone, and tuba) is also rather common. A lot of good music exists for the group.

(e) Various sextets, septets, octets, etc., are written for winds, also. After 9 or 10 instruments, the piece loses its number-designating title, and is likely to be *Opus X for Small Wind Band.*

The American "Swing Band"

In the 1930s and 1940s, the jazz band supreme was a whopping big crowd known universally as a big band. Benny Goodman, Count Basie, Tommy Dorsey, and hundreds of others made the Big Band an international hit with jazz lovers. Typically, a big band consisted of 4-5 saxophones, 3-4 trumpets, 1-3 trombones, piano, string bass, guitar, drums, boy singer, girl singer, and small vocal group. The band was capable of playing everything from the most languid, warm ballad love song to the most aggressive jack-hammer ear-splitting "up tune."

Rather often, a small group would be extracted from the big band to offer some variety throughout the night: Benny Goodman had a trio, quartet, and a sextet; Tommy Dorsey had the Clambake Seven; Bob Crosby had the Bobcats; Artie Shaw had the Gramercy Five. Sometimes the small groups worked as individual show units, sometimes they appeared out front while the big band played along in back of them in a musical dialogue.

This same kind of interplay between a small group and a large group existed in the Baroque Era (1600-1750) in an operation called the *concerto grosso*, with a little group known as the *concertino* churning away in opposition and cooperation with a big group known as the *ripieno.*

More about the concerto grosso, later. The point here is that Benny Goodman and the Baroque composers were both responding to the same instinctive urge to delight themselves and their audiences with the fun of trading musical ideas between small and large forces. Dramatic interplay is always an interesting and satisfying musical technique.

The Traditional Dixieland Band

Since the early 1900s when they first appeared, Dixieland bands have come in and out of style every 10 years or so. Louis Armstrong, Pete Fountain, and a few others have made a good living playing Dixieland jazz consistently through all the various style changes in popular music. A Dixieland group will have, generally, six core instruments: piano, drums, string bass (tuba, in the old days), trumpet (cornet, for the purists), trombone, and clarinet.

MISCELLANEOUS ENSEMBLES
The Brass Choir
Colleges and universities frequently have a group of anywhere from 12 to 20 musicians specializing in the performance of high quality music written exclusively for brass instruments. The instrumentation, the music, and the whole approach is very much like the brass section out of the symphony orchestra.
The Guitar Ensemble
On the rise in universities. Several guitarists, all playing classical acoustic guitars, will present an entire evening of intimate chamber music. With solos, duets, trios, and now and then a larger combined effort, the guitar ensemble can create a full evening of beautifully subtle aesthetic pleasures.
The Percussion Ensemble
In the past 20 years, an ensemble of exotic percussion instruments has grown up in the professional world and in university music departments. With an increasing body of music written specifically for its instruments, the percussion ensemble is getting more satisfying and convincing as a musical experience as time progresses. Besides the traditional drums, gongs, triangles, etc., there will be brake drums, pyrex kitchen bowls, beads, rattles, egg beaters, hunks of tin, and everything imaginable—including for melodic purposes, the piano, if needed, and xylophones, marimbas, glockenspiels—the works.
The Wind Ensemble
Many colleges have a select group of winds called the wind ensemble. Its purpose is to play a more esoteric repertory than can the large band. Wind ensembles do not march or perform in any other setting but the formal concert stage, as a general rule, and they dress like a symphony orchestra might dress, with tuxedos for the men and long black dresses for the ladies. The entire intent and effect is very much like a symphony for winds.

The Collegium Musicum
        Historical roots is the name of the game, here, with instruments, music, costumes, and all coming right out of the Middle Ages and Renaissance. Heady stuff, indeed, of great meaning for musicologists, but not terribly big with average Americans. In the early 1970s, though, with John Renbourn, Pentangle, and some others digging into the Middle Ages for new songs and sounds, the Collegium Musicum generated a new interest on college campuses.

Pre-Recorded Mixtures
        Disney-on-Parade, Ice Shows, theme-park revue shows, and many other of America's new musical activities carry banks of tapes for large portions of their music. The traveling shows often move into town with only a conductor, pianist, and drummer. Eight or ten horns are then hired from the local musicians, and the whole package is put together with the pre-recorded string section for a complete sound. The conductor works from a "click track," and keeps everything coordinted by matching his beat pattern to clicks which he hears but which are not audible to anyone else.
                                    *****
        This list of instrumental groups is by no means complete. There are many more: polka bands, jug bands, be-bop combos, cocktail trios, mariachi bands, steel-drum bands, hand bell choirs, old-timey mountain string groups, blues bands, and dozens of variations on these basic themes. Each group speaks with authority and beauty to its particular audience because the audience and the musicians undersand the common musical language of the entire experience. They share the "meaning" of the music, and agree at a subliminal level that this is the way life is and ought to be.

9

Instrumental Forms

Chapter Seven, "Principles of Multi-Unit Musical Form", discussed how music is organized for a large experience. This chapter will examine those special forms for instruments which follow the principles of multi-unit organization—the suite, the Baroque sonata, the Baroque concerto, the Baroque overture, the sonata form-at-large, the concerto grosso—and two forms which are not really multi-unit operations, but rather multi-sectional forms, the overture and the symphonic poem.

Multi-unit instrumental forms will often have a short break of dead silence between the movements. No one applauds during this little silent pause. Please note—no one applauds between movements of these large works. On rare occasions, perhaps, after an especially good movement, applause will break out spontaneously because the movement

ILLUSTRATION: The LaSalle Quartet. From left to right—Walter Levin, Henry Meyer, Lee Fiser, Peter Kamnitzer. Courtesy of the LaSalle Quartet.

was simply so extraordinarily well done that it deserved special, instant, recognition. The general rule is, however, do not applaud. Most people feel that any kind of applause between the movements would break the aesthetic thread of the work as a whole. This is why the tradition grew.

THE SUITE
The term means "collection" (from an Old French word for the staff [retinue] of attendants to a person of noble rank), and the term is used in several ways: a suite of furniture, a suite of executive offices, a bridal suite (several rooms), and so on. In music, suites are sometimes created out of all new material, but often created from music already written for a ballet, opera, Broadway show, movie or television score, or set of dance tunes.

Early Suites
In the 1500s and early 1600s European composers, following the practice of performing musicians, began to link certain dances in sequential delivery. In time, 6 to 10 individual pieces might appear as a kind of unit-at-large. By the late 1600s and early 1700s, a rather predictable scheme emerged. There are hundreds of exceptions, to be sure, but the following is considered by scholars to be a classical model. The dances were nearly always in binary form.

(1) *Allemande.* A German dance. Quadruple meter. Somber. Frequently with a "pick-up note." Often ornamented with grace notes, trills, etc.

(2) *Courante.* French origin. Triple meter. Accents (stresses) shift from ONE-two-three, ONE-two-three to ONE-two-THREE, one-TWO-three, occasionally. Contrapuntal.

(3) *Sarabande.* Spanish dance. Triple meter. Dignified. Accent or long note often on count two, thus one-TWO-three. Considered a wild and lascivious dance in its early days.

(4) Option open here for any number of dance forms: minuet, bourree, passapied, polonaise, air, loure, rigaudon, and others.

(5) *Gigue.* British origin. Six-eight meter. Fugal opening. Second half of the piece was frequently an inversion of the first half. Dotted rhythms.

During the Renaissance (1450-1600) and earlier, these dances had been real dances by real people in real life situations, lower-class dances, often. These dances became stylized art products during the Baroque Period (1600-1750) and later. As Marshall McLuhan said, "The older technologies, the older environment, become the content of the new environmental technology." In this case, the life circumstances of social dancing became the art forms of later generations. Today, following McLuhan's principle, blue denim, a hard core utilitarian clothing material in the early 1900s, has become a fashionable stylish plaything, for everything from cowboy flavored single breasted suits to decorative interior fabric for automobiles.

Back to the musical discipline. If a composer in the year 2001 were to write a dance suite based on dance forms of the 1950s and 1960s, the collection might appear as an Alligator, a Frug, a Mashed Potato, and optional dance (perhaps a Charleston, just to go back into a previous culture period—for the sheer novelty of doing so), and conclude with a Watusi. A disco dance might be too new to be included. A certain historical distance is necessary before the process seems to occur.

The *French Suite No. 6 in E* by Johann Sebastian Bach (1685-1750) provides a good model for the Baroque Suite in a typical appearance.

French Suite in E, by Johann Sebastian Bach

(1)	Allemande	1:49
(2)	Courante	:50
(3)	Sarabande	1:17
(4)	Gavotte	:36
(5)	Polonaise	:49
(6)	Bourree	:58
(7)	Minuet	:31
(8)	Gigue	1:15
	Total Musical Time	8:05

Why would J. S. Bach, church organist and choir director, write a suite in the year 1723? Many reasons: as instruction pieces for his pupils (his own children among them), to have some new music to play, to impress someone who might offer him a better job at a larger church for more money, to sell the music to some musicians who needed something to perform. All the normal reasons why people write music, today.

Why are the pieces still heard in recitals and concerts today? Because they are a satisfying and fulfilling way to spend 8-10 minutes in sound. Why the contrasting sections? For variety. To foil fatigue. Just as surely as Kenny Rogers knows how to vary the works on a concert, a Baroque composer knew how to cast up these sounds so they unfold in a pleasing manner.

Later Suites

After the Baroque Period, music was still offered in collections, but the collection might be called a divertimento, or cassation, or serenade, or it might still be called a suite, or it might be called a *partita*. Composers were not, and are not, very tidy about these things at all. Mozart's *Serenade No. 10 in B-flat Major* (K. 361) is really a suite. Also Mendelssohn's *Midsummer Night's Dream*, and Tchaikovsky's *Nutcracker Suite*, of course.

Modern rock musicians are having some fun with suites, too. Emerson, Lake, and Palmer tried their hand at a suite from the Romantic Period (1820-1900), *Pictures at an Exhibition*, by Modest Mussorgsky (1839-1881). Mussorgsky wrote the work after viewing an exhibition of sketches by his friend, Victor Hartmann. Hartmann had just died, and the exhibition was put together in his honor by his friends. Mussorgsky was deeply moved by the pictures, and set out immediately to capture his feelings in music, as a tribute to Hartmann.

What most people do not know is that the whole thing was originally written for piano. It was transcribed for orchestra by the French composer Maurice Ravel, and this version for orchestra is the most common appearance of the work in concert.

Each of five different treatments of *Pictures* creates a slightly different musical experience.

(a) The original piano composition. Bernard Ringeissen, pianist. Musical Heritage Records. Catalog No. 1788.

(b) The orchestra transcription of the above. Thomas Schippers, conductor. New York Philharmonic Orchestra. Columbia Odyssey 32-16-0376.

(c) A rock version. Emerson, Lake, and Palmer. Cotillion Elp 66666. Selected items from the suite.

(d) An electronic version. Isao Tomita, composer-performer of electronic synthesizer music. RCA Red Seal Stereo ARL 1-0838.

(e) A version for solo acoustic guitar. Kazuhito Yamashita, guitarist. RCA Real Seal (Digital) ARC1-4203 Stereo.

The organization of the suite (according to Martin Last's version of Alfred Frankenstein's descriptive summary) follows below. Ten items with a promenade as connective tissue.

Pictures at an Exhibition

Modest Mussorgsky

**Promenade. The composer wanders through the Hartmann memorial exhibit, examining the curious drawings of his deceased artist-architect friend.

(1) The Gnome. Hartmann's drawing represents a little gnome walking on his deformed legs. The sketch is really a design for a toy nutcracker.

**Promenade, again. Sometimes Mussorgsky promenades between pictures, and sometimes he goes directly from picture to picture.

(2) The Old Castle. A medieval castle and a melancholy troubadour. This particularly entry does not occur in the Hartmann catalog, but Mussorgsky's conception is thought to derive from a set of architectural drawings Hartmann did in Italy.

**Promenade.

(3) Tuileries. Noisy children with their nurses in the famed Paris park create a lot of noise.

(4) Bydalo. An enormous, ponderous, Polish watan, drawn by Oxen, lumbers across the landscape.

**Promenade.

(5) Ballet of the Unhatched Chicks. Hartmann's sketch was of canaries, tightly enclosed in shells that resemble suits of armor. This sketch is really a design for a costume intended for a ballet called "Trilbi."

(6) Samuel Goldenberg and Schmuyle. Two Jewish merchants, one wealthy and the other poor, are wrangling in a business deal. After the pompous rich man has his say, the poor merchant responds in a high-pitched complaint. Then they argue at the same time.

(7) The Market Place at Limoges. Women at the Limoges market squabble, gossip, and fuss at each other.

(8) Catacombs. Hartmann's water color showed the artist himself and a friend going through the catacombs of Paris with a guide holding the lamp.

(9) The Hut on Fowls' Legs. Baba Yaga, a shaman-witch of Russian folklore, is believed to live in a hut with appendages like chickens' legs.

(10) The Great Gate at Kiev. A musical portrait of the proposed great gate (never built) which Hartmann had sketched out several times.

Modern Suites

Jazz, rock, and comtemporary classical composers have been turning out suites for many years now. Witness Leonard Bernstein's *On The Waterfront* Symphonic Suite from his movie score; Dimitri Kabalevsky's *Comedians*, ten little units from a theater work; Aaron Copland's *Rodeo* ballet suite; Duke Ellington's *Drum is a Woman*; Bill Chase's *Invitation to a River*; and dozens of other suites.

All in all, the suite—whether conceived for harpsichord in 1723, or for an orchestra in 1872, or for a jazz-rock recording date in the 1980s—turns out to be a rewarding and fulfilling way to cast up an extended musical experience.

SONATA

The term comes from the Italian verb *suonare* ("to sound"), thus, in its original use, a sonata was a "sound piece," that is, a piece to be sounded on a wind or stringed instrument; not to be confused with toccata, from *toccare* ("to touch"), for a keyboard instrument; not to be confused with cantata, from *cantare* ("to sing"), that is, a piece to be sung. The terms have lost their original meaning (except for the term cantata which still means a piece which will be sung), and today pianists perform sonatas and brass instrumentalists perform toccatas.

Early Sonatas

Collection Principle. European composers began to use the term sonata for short instrumental works in the early 1500s. Throughout the Baroque (1600-1750), the term referred to a multi-movement work for a small group of instrumentalists. Several sections, anywhere from 3 to 7, often, may or may not be decisively separated. Many varieties appeared: Chamber sonatas (known as the *sonata de camera*) much like a suite; church sonatas (known as the *sonata da chiesa*), more solemn than chamber sonatas; and *trio sonatas* (three separate parts, but played by four instruments).

Later Sonatas

Pattern Principle. By the time of the Classic Period (1750-1820), the term sonata begins to mean something very specific: a composition for a solo instrument. If that instrument is a keyboard instrument, the work will, in fact, be a solo operation. If that instrument is a single-line melodic instrument (flute, clarinet, trumpet, violin), the musical offering will be supported by an accompanying keyboard instrument. Thus, a Beethoven piano sonata will be for piano alone, but a Beethoven violin sonata will be for violin with piano accompaniment. The large scale formal design of the sonata during the Classic and most of the Romantic Period will be described under the heading Sonata Form-at-Large.

Modern Sonatas

The term is used loosely, these days, and often indicates some kind of pattern principal at work, but not always. Vincent Persichetti's *Third Piano Sonata* has three movements: Declaration, Episode, and Hymn. Paul Hindemith wrote several sonatas in, roughly, the traditional mold of the sonata form-at-large. Jazz and rock musicians use the term sparingly, with no precise meaning clearly consistent throughout the music industry today, except, perhaps, that whatever gets called a sonata will be an instrumental, not a vocal, work.

CONCERTO

From the Italian verb *concertare* (roughly, "to do battle [fight side by side] as compatriots"), thus, a concerto is a piece with two musical forces at work.

Early Concertos

The term concerto goes all the way back to the late 1500s when it was used to refer to vocal works with instrumental accompaniment. Indeed, well into the Baroque Period (1600-1750), the term can be found for what were essentially cantatas.

Near the end of the Baroque Period (1600-1750), the term concerto begins to mean something based on the collection principle, and the term appears on many different kinds of multi-movement instrumental works (spiritual concertos, solo concertos, concerto-sinfonias, and others) with, generally, some kind of contrasting musical ingredients as part of the aesthetic experience. A special kind of Baroque concerto, the concerto grosso, became quite popular.

In a concerto grosso, two groups of musicians are pitted against and work with each other: (a) a small group called the *concertino*, or *principale*, or *soli*, consisting of two or three melody instruments, and (b) a large group of musicians called the *ripieno*, or *concerto*, or *tutti* consisting of a small string orchestra, 6-9 strings, with, occasionally, a few wind instruments of the day, plus what was called the *continuo*, or *basso continuo*, or *thorough-bass* (harpsichord and cello—a "rhythm section," as the jazz musician would call it).

The real fun of all this lay in the sheer sportive joy of the interplay between the little group and the big group—kind of like America in 1939 with the Benny Goodman Trio out in front of his big band, everyone contributing, alternately and in ensemble, to the full musical offering. The same musical instincts are being served here in two different historical-cultural circumstances.

Early concerto grossos were written in 5-7 movements, but later works by Antonio Vivaldi (1675-1743) established a three-movement design which became a kind of standard: allegro (fast), adagio (slow), and allegro (fast), during which, in the fast movements especially, there is a lot of alternating between the small and large forces, as in, for example, Vivaldi's *Concerto Grosso in D-minor, Op. 3, No. 11*.

Later Concertos

Pattern Principle. As with the sonata, the term concerto takes on a rather specific meaning in the Classic Period (1750-1820): a composition for solo instrument with an orchestra providing an accompaniment. Mozart's famous clarinet concerto, thus, is a work for a clarinet and orchestra.

The large scale formal design of the concerto during the Classic Period and later is rather clearly defined, and will be described now under the following heading, Sonata Form-at-Large.

SONATA FORM-AT-LARGE

Pattern Principle. The term was coined by music historian Willi Apel to clarify the multiple uses of the word sonata in the music field. "Sonata form" might mean three different things: one, the exposition-development-recapitulation form discussed in Chapter Six, page 54; two, the term for a piece for violin, with piano accompainment, mentioned, above (pp. 79-80); three, the term for a large-scale multi-movement work for instruments. It is best to clarify by using *sonata-allegro design* for the first meaning; *sonata* for the second meaning; and *sonata form-at-large* for the third meaning.

Sonata form-at-large works appear during the Classic Period (1750-1820), and are very big and important through most of the Romantic Period (1820-1900), continuing often well into the 20th Century. The form is one of the great contributions of Judaic-Christian Culture to world art.

Organizational Scheme

Movement I	Brisk "allegro" tempo. Almost always in sonata-allegro design (see Chapter Six, page 54).
Movement II	Slow tempo. Theme-and-variations, or, sometimes, ternary form, or, sometimes, a slow rondo. Many different single-unit designs were used (see Chapter Six).
Movement III	Dance tempo, moderate. Minuet-Trio[-Minuet] was used for a long time, until Beethoven began using a Scherzo-Trio[-Scherzo] in its place.
Movement IV	Fast tempo. Another sonata-allegro design, perhaps. Or a rondo. Or something else which would permit the composer to go out with a flourish (see Chapter Six for rondo form).

Species

Four different species of the above grand organizational scheme crystallized during the Classic Period, each of which was (theoretically) in the above prescribed four-movement pattern.

**(1) *Sonata*. A composition for a single instrument. If a keyboard instrument, then alone. If for a melody instrument—violin, clarinet, flute, and such—then with keyboard accompaniment, usually piano.

**(2) *concerto*. A composition for a single instrument with orchestra. The instrumentalist and the orchestra work with and against each other in a manner similar to the large and small groups in the concerto grosso.

During the sonata-allegro designs in a concerto, the opening sections will often be a double exposition—meaning that the orchestra will open with the first and second themes of the design (see Chapter Six), and then the solo instrumentalist will deliver the first and second themes.

(3) *Chamber Works*. Compositions for string quartets, woodwind quintets, string trios, piano quartets (a piano plus three strings, [usually cello, violin, and viola]), and similar works.

(4) *Symphony*. A composition for a full orchestra. Mozart's *Symphony No. 40 in G-minor* might call for only 30-40 instruments, for example, while Beethoven's *Symphony No. 7 in A* might call for 70 or more instruments.

** In sonatas and concertos, the composer would often omit what would have been a third movement. Composers are extremely sensitive to psychoemotional time and interest-fatigue factors, and, by intuition, they will do as much as possible to sustain maximum interest in their music. They feel, perhaps, that without the grand sweep of colors and dynamics available to them in a larger group of musicians, they had better shorten their concertos and sonatas a little to hold their listener's attention.

A sonata, then, is a sonata form-at-large for a single instrument. A concerto is a sonata form-at-large for a solo instrument with orchestra accompaniment. Chamber works are sonata forms-at-large for small groups. A symphony is a sonata form-at-large for an entire orchestra.

A rather famous melody occurs in one of Wolfgang Mozart's sonatas—his *Sonata in C, K. 545*, for solo piano. The

"K." is for Ludwig von Koechel, a German scientist who was a Mozart scholar. Koechel catalogued all of Mozart's works in what he believed to be the proper chronological order. In 1937, Alfred Einstein revised Koechel's listing of 1862.

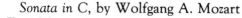

Sonata in C, by Wolfgang A. Mozart
(1) First Movement

Theme I

Theme II

(2) Second Movement

(3) Third Movement

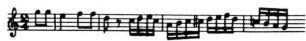

OVERTURE

Sometimes multi-movement, sometimes not, but included here because of its large dimensions. Generally, the word overture is used to indicate that the piece is conceived as an introductory statement, a kind of preface to some larger musical operation, an opera, ballet, or Broadway show, for example. Quite often, the larger work has been forgotten while the overture lingers on as a fulfilling concert piece on its own (like the famous overture to Rossini's opera *William Tell*). Quite often, also, overtures are written as straight out concert offerings of their own, not meant to be introductory to anything else.

Overtures are not really multi-movement works, but rather multi-sectional works. The pause between sections is not as long as the pause between movements as in, say, a full symphony. Between symphony movements the musicians might quickly check the tuning of their instruments, the trumpet player will blow the saliva out of his horn, the conductor will mop his brow, and the audience will squirm around into new seating positions. Not so in an overture. Between sections of an overture no one moves; indeed, the conductor will often keep his baton held high at a kind of "attention" position to ensure that the pause will in fact be short and that the continuous spell of the overture-as-a-whole will not be broken.

Early Overtures

Collection Principle. Two kinds appear regularly in the late 1600s and early 1700s:

French Overture. In two sections—the first, a slow section with dotted rhythms; the second, a fast contrapuntal section which ends, often, with a short, slow, broad coda-like concluding gestue.

Italian Overture. Sometimes called *sinfonia.* Three sections: allegro (fast), adagio (slow), and allegro (fast). All movements in simple homophonic style except the first, which has some imitative entrances in the opening passages.

The overture to the *Messiah*, a famous oratorio, by George Frederick Handel (1685-1759) is a splendid example of a French overture.

Overture to *Messiah*, by G. F. Handel

(1) First Section

(2) Second Section

Later Overtures

Many are introductory works which set the mood for what is to come, like Mozart's overture to the *Marriage of*

Figaro. Many are straight-forward concert pieces, like Tchaikovsky's *1812 Overture* and Brahms' *Academic Festival Overture*. Many are a kind of potpourri of the most memorable melodies from the show to come.

Modern Overtures

Jazz and rock musicians use the term overture in the traditional sense, usually. Peter Townshend's overture to *Tommy*, for instance, is a classic declaration of the mood and substance of things to come in the opera, along with snatches of the more memorable melodies in store. Townshend apparently knew precisely what he was doing, because midway in the opera, right after the gypsy acid queen sings her song, "I'm the gypsy—the acid queen/Pay before we start," he presents a section called *Underture*. It is a near ten minute instrumental section designed, quite obviously, to represent in music the effects of the drug trip Tommy is on.

Generally speaking, the term overture is used these days for a straight-out instrumental piece. *Overture*, by Blood, Sweat, and Tears, for example. Or the overture to *My Fair Lady*, as fragments of melodies to come later in the show. Classical composers most often use the term for a concert piece: William Schuman's *American Festival Overture*, Aaron Copland's *Outdoor Overture*, and Shostakovich's *Festive Overture* are typical of the form.

SYMPHONIC POEM

A multi-sectional instrumental work without, usually, any discernible break in the overall aesthetic sweep. The work comes off as an organic whole even though the differences between and among the sections create wide changes of mood. During the Romantic Period, composers began to get their inspiration for writing big orchestral works from outside the musical field—from poetry, painting, philosophy, literature, and religion—and they cast up their works in one grand all-inclusive nonstop delivery, 20-30 minutes long. Contrasting sections exist within, of course, but the whole composition is presented as one continuous musical experience.

The title may or may not be a guide, incidentally. Claude Debussy's *Prelude to the Afternoon of a Faun* is not a prelude but a symphonic poem. Tchaikovsky's overture *Romeo and Juliet* is not an overture but a symphonic poem. By its very nature, the symphonic poem elicits a colorful name: *Through the Looking Glass*, Deems Taylor; *The Sea*, Claude Debussy; *Death and Transfiguration*, Richard Strauss; *George Washington Bridge*, William Schuman.

Modern jazz and rock musicians have taken two directions on the symphonic poem (sometimes called, also, a tone poem). First, they have simply created large compositions which are indeed symphonic poems even if not so indicated in the title or on the record jacket. Miles Davis, Freddie Hubbard, and many others have single compositions 18-20 minutes long quite often on their recordings. These works are partly improvised, partly scored, and are, therefore, perfectly consistent with the jazz tradition. The intent is quite clearly to capture the full spirit and emotional feel of a grand theme/idea/mood, and that is what a symphonic poem is all about.

Second, the jazz and rock musicians have sensed instinctively that they are spiritual compatriots with the Romantic composers of symphonic poems, and they (the jazz-rock-fusion crowd) have boldly dipped into traditional symphonic poems to extract certain musical ideas—sometimes taking the original work almost intact—for the creation of their own jazz-rock version of the work. Eumir Deodato's treatment of Strauss' *Also Sprach Zarathustra* (2001) created much interest in 1973. And later, Bob James' version of Mussorgsky's *Night on Bald Mountain* and Hubert Laws' rendition of Tchaikovsky's *Romeo and Juliet*.

As jazz and rock musicians tackle more ambitious projects, it seems likely that their efforts will result in modern symphonic poems, and the alternate term, tone poem, may come into more frequent use to describe these large-scale operations.

CONCEPT ALBUM

Another successful jazz-rock effort to deliver a large scale musical experience is the concept album, an album with a central idea holding all selections together. Most concept albums are really song cycles, and are discussed in Chapter Thirteen, "Large Secular Forms For Voices". A few rare items might be considered instrumental concept albums, *Tarkus*, by Emerson, Lake and Palmer, for example, and perhaps also *Trilogy*.

MISCELLANEOUS TITLES FOR INSTRUMENTAL COMPOSITIONS

Many of the titles listed below come from the Romantic Period when composers tried to give their works a poetic name which would somehow suggest the emotional character of the musical experience. Composers of piano pieces were especially fond of doing this, so in the absence of specific remarks to the contrary, the titles listed below will be piano works, "character pieces" as they are called in the trade.

Nearly all of the works will be in some rough kind of A-B-A (ternary) form also. Ternary form, however, loosely developed, has a deep satisfaction about it which is all the Romantics really wanted in the way of formal design. The romantic composers made a special effort to avoid clear-cut delineation of architectural principles in their music.

Arabesque. A short composition with a good deal of decorative and intricate filigree.

Badinerie. A playful, humorous composition.

Bagatelle. A short piece of undefined character, generally light.

Ballade. A highly dramatic work.

Barcarole. A lilting piece which suggests the rocking motion of a boat.

Berceuse. A cradle song, or lullaby.

Cassation. Probably a suite conceived to be played outdoors by a small orchestra. Practically the same as a *divertimento* or a *serenade*.

Chorale fantasia. An organ composition in which the basic chorale (hymn tune) is given a very free improvisatory treatment.

Chorale partita. Variations for organ on a chorale (hymn tune).

Chorale prelude. An organ composition designed to be played before the congregation sings the hymn.

Divertimento. See cassation.

Eclogue. A composition of idyllic, pastoral nature.

Ecossiase. A kind of quick dance-like tune in 2/4 meter.

Elegy. A plaintive, sad composition.

Entr'acte. A piece performed between opera acts, an orchestral piece.

Etude. A piece for study, but often sufficiently musical to be performed in recital or concert.

Fanfare. A short tune for brass instruments used as an introductory statement for ceremonial music.

Fantasia. A piece which is either highly improvisatory or highly delicate and dream-like.

Habanera. A Cuban dance in slow duple meter with syncopated figures.

Humoresque. An instrumental composition of whimsical character.

Impromptu. A composition supposedly conceived in an off-handed manner by the composer.

Interlude. A short piece inserted between other works.

Intermezzo. A piece composed by a composer between major works. Thus, somewhat lighter than a composer's output of the period. Also, an *entr'acte.*

Intrada. An opening piece, overture-like.

Invention. A short, highly contrapuntal piece.

March. Two kinds: a composition for actual marching, military style; and a composition for concert performance in march or quasi-march style.

Mazurka. A Polish national dance, in triple meter.

Nocturne. Night piece, thus, somewhat languid.

Ode. A poetic musical statement.

Partita. Either a suite or a set of theme and variations.

Potpourri. A medley (collection) of popular tunes which are delivered without a break.

Prelude. Technically, a piece to be played as an introduction to something else. Preludes exist, though, quite often, as independent works, and also as the front half of a double package of musical materials—like Prelude and Fugue.

Quadrille. A French dance, alternating between 6/8 and 2/4 meters.

Rag. A piano composition, early jazz style, usually in two distinct sections which probably resemble a traditional military march schematic design.

Rhapsody. A free imaginative musical composition.

Serenade. Cassation or divertimento. Also, a love song.

Toccata. A keyboard piece of somewhat free virtuosic dimensions. Also a piece for brass instruments.

Voluntary. An organ piece to be played at a church service.

Waltz. A piece in 3/4 meter.

BALLET

Nearly always, the music exists or is conceived first, then the appropriate bodily gestures envisioned, demonstrated, and taught to the troupe of dancers. There is no ballet "form," in musical terms, like sonata or ternary design. Ballet music tends to be either (a) a collection of things like a suite, or (b) a large scale mood piece like a symphonic poem.

The dancing art, itself, comes in two major divisions, each with some subdivisions. First, the classical tradition, in three levels.

(1) Classical ballet is the highest, most abstract, and most esoteric of all dance forms, to be sure. With the ballerinas on the tips of their hard-toe slippers and the male dancers in classic tights, this is pure artistic motion without scenery, story line, or any other extraneous factors whatsoever.

(2) Modern ballet admits to a story line, or an interpretation of a mood, or some kind of descriptive effort by the dancers. It is, thus, slightly less formalized and less purely abstract than classical ballet.

(3) Modern dance will probably not be executed in the classical ballet attire, and will be very directly related to the show. The dance sequences in Bernstein's *West Side Story* for example.

Second, the commercial-folk tradition, in three levels.

(1) Folk dancing is still alive and well, with high school and college students occasionally digging back into their ancestors' pleasures for jigs, Virginia reels, and square dancing parties.

(3) Night-club dancing—by whatever name: ballroom, Charleston, jitterbug, Twist, boogie, disco, reggae—is a kind of special ritual in Western Civilization. No other culture has quite the same thing. The age of "Classical Ballroom" would certainly be the 1930s and 1940s with Fred Astaire and Ginger Rogers leading the way.

(3) Commercial styles will be around for a long time in the form of tap dancers, soft shoe specialists, strip-tease artists, **chorus-line revues, Westernized belly dancers, and the like.**

ILLUSTRATION: Ballet dancers in performance. Courtesy of the CCM Publicity Office, Cincinnati, Ohio.

Part IV
Voices and
Vocal-Choral
Forms

10

Voice Classification And Singing Styles

There must be thousands of ways to produce sounds which would be described as "singing" by one culture or another throughout the world, and each style has great beauty and meaning for those who produce and consume it. It is a deep-seated cultural thing, however, and anyone outside the culture will probably have a hard time "appreciating" it. An Eskimo whale-hunting tune will not do much for an opera fan; nor will the quartet scene from *Rigoletto* do much for an Alaskan Eskimo.

The same kind of closed-door aesthetic problems exist within a given culture—American society, for example. The sound of an operatic soprano is a pretty funny thing to most school children, whatever their socioeconomic background. And Mick Jagger's voice did not find many kindly ears among the board members of America's opera companies. The whole

ILLUSTRATION: Italo Tajo, Basso-in-residence, University of Cincinnati's College-Conservatory of Music, in the role of Figaro. Courtesy of Mr. Tajo.

business of singing styles and vocal sounds is very complex, indeed.

Singing is an intensely personal expression, but it is an even more intense social ritual. It reveals sociocultural assumptions and attitudes which are sometimes revealed in no other way. Not only the song texts, which are a complete study in themselves, but the sound of the voices reveal and celebrate deep-seated cultural beliefs. In American society, several major vocal styles are clearly evident.[1]

COUNTRY VOICES
A dozen varieties exist, to be sure, but two large divisions come immediately to mind.

Raw-Boned Pure Country
Jean Ritchie, Roy Acuff, Buck Owens, Ernest Tubb, Webb Pierce, George Jones, Willie Nelson, and many others. Some very successful, commercially, some not so successful. The sound is nasal, pain-filled, and loaded with emotional meaning for millions of America's country music fans. The tunes are straight ahead Anglo-Celtic statements on love, cheating, religion, drinking, and down home conservative views of reality.

Pop Country
Barbara Mandrell, Dolly Parton, Crystal Gayle, Tanya Tucker, and others, nearly all big commercial successes because they have somehow held on to their purist country fans while reaching out into a pop market. The sound is less restricted, more open and resonant, with a slower and wider vibrato, and less obviously locked into mountain culture. They are still a long way from Frank Sinatra or Julie Andrews, but the pop country singers have moved judiciously in that direction.

AFRO-AMERICAN VOICES
Black voices. On rare occasion, though, a few white singers will absorb the emotional spirit so convincingly that they really belong here: Jack Teagarden, Mel Torme, and Peggy Lee. The style and sub-styles are endless, but again (as with country music) two major divisions are everywhere apparent.

Down-Home Shouters

Two subcategories, here: (a) the gospel and spiritual area, and (b) the blues area. Many singers start out in gospel and shift over into the secular stuff: James Brown and Aretha Franklin. For all their electric backgrounds (synthesizers, ring modulators, tone dividers, and such), the disco singers really belong here, too; Donna Summer, for example.

Sophisticated Jazz

Ella Fitzgerald, Sarah Vaughan, Carmen McRae, Eddie Jefferson. Some white singers, here, too: Mark Murphy, Anita O'Day, June Christy, Peggy Lee, Mel Torme, and a few others. The sound is much more refined, less pain-filled, and free of the open-wound emotional discharge so characteristic of the blues and gospel shouters.

MAINSTREAM AMERICAN POP
Broadway-Based Show Pop

Al Jolson, Ethel Merman, Eddie Cantor, right up to Bette Midler and Barbra Streisand. The sound is brilliant, metallic, penetrating, with a narrow and fast vibrato—deriving, perhaps, from the sound of the cantors in Old-World synagogues. A unique and expressive sound which is quite peculiar to the Eastern Seaboard in America.

Middle-of-the-Road Pop

Andy Williams, Perry Como, Bing Crosby and hundreds of others. The sound is pleasant, comfortable, resonant, less nervous than the Broadway voice, and delivered in the middle range of the voice, quite often. A good number of the mainstream pop singers come out of deeper, more clearly ethnic-centered, musical environs. Nat Cole came out of jazz. Glenn Campbell out of country music. John Denver out of folk music.

ROCK

How many categories? At the risk of over-simplification and over-generalization, two categories, again.

Pure-Energy Rock

Mick Jagger, Janis Joplin, and second generation rock disciples. These voices are a cultural mix of gospel-shouting black and pain-wracked country, often twice transplanted to British soil and back to America.

Pop Rock

Karen Carpenter, Helen Reddy, and similar voices. This kind of singing will become the MOR in a few years. The sound of the voice, the topics, the instrumental background—all is non-threatening and gentle. These singers will become the next generations of Bing Crosby, Doris Day, Dinah Shore, Merv Griffin, and similar "personalities"— movies, TV shows, and all.

All this classification of voices and singing styles is grossly drawn, of course. There are dozens of big-name singers in the business who do not fit very well into any of the above four categories. What about Kenny Rogers? Natalie Cole? Generally, they all started out in a rather pure category, then moved with their careers to a kind of middle territory in the forest of fine singers.

The purpose of the classification is, after all, to identify some of the areas of trees throughout the forest, not to drive a nail into every single little sapling. Life is too beautifully complex to force every singer into this arbitrarily contrived classification. Best now to push on to the really complicated category of voices and singing styles.

CLASSICAL VOICES

Classical singing employs a highly sophisticated system of resonating principles, with the sound being amplified and honed into focus and clarity through the upper regions of the chest and throught he sinus-nasal cavities. It takes years and years of rigorous training before some singers even understand and finally "feel" what this is all about. Moreover, after the technique is acquired, it tends to go out of adjustment rather easily, and like a four-barrel carburetor, it needs constant attention to keep things working at maximum efficiency. Most big-league opera singers have a personal voice teacher who keeps them tuned up—not so much for musical interpretations as for vocal production techniques. Their career depends on it.

Classical singers are generally grouped into six ranges, with four quality-style attributes. First the ranges.

Female Voices.
(1) *Soprano.* The highest female voice range. The leading lady who dies in the arms of her lover in the final act of the opera.
(2) *Mezzo-Soprano.* Medium range. The leading lady's maid, or good friend, who delivers the secret note which proves that the lover has been seen in the arms of another woman.
(3) *Contralto.* Lowest female voice range. She may or may not be in the opera. Or she may be the leading lady's maid, in which case the mezzo-soprano is probably the other woman.

Male Voices
(4) *Tenor.* The highest male voice range. The hero in the opera. He's the good guy and has one of the most demanding roles.
(5) *Baritone.* Medium range. Villain or villain's accomplice.
(6) *Bass.* Lowest male voice. The villain, or the magistrate, or the leading lady's father.

This classification is not as clear cut as it appears. It is not based on range (how high or low the vocalist can sing) alone. It has to do with the "quality" or sound of the voice, as well. There are some baritones who can sing as high as the tenors, but they are really baritones—the voice is thicker and darker than a tenor's voice. There are some tenors who cannot sing too high, but the sound is still very definitely that of a tenor classification—light, clear, and free from those dark shadings so characteristic of the baritones and basses.

Also, and this is a terribly complex and frustrating thing for singers to experience, some singers actually change from, say, tenor to baritone or from baritone to tenor as they emerge from early manhood to full maturity. Voice teachers are constantly on the alert to be sure that they are not doing grave damage to a young man who has been singing (and even sounding) like a tenor for years, but who is really a baritone with an unusually high top to his range. Music schools are full of young singers who may respond to an innocent question, "What are you?" by saying, "My teacher things I'm a mezzo-soprano, but we're not sure yet. I auditioned as a lyric soprano."

All of which has enormous consequence for a singer. Changing from one classification to another is more than just learning to "feel" a different set of acoustic-muscular principles at work; it means learning a whole new repertory of songs, and dreaming a whole new set of dreams about future career development. Small wonder that young classical singers are a nervous and high-strung crowd.

It is even more complex. There are four (theoretical) quality-color distinctions within each of the above six general categories.

(a) *The Coloratura Voice.* Light, delicate, agile, crystal clear, capable of rapid passages and runs and trills.
(b) *The Lyric Voice.* Pure, poetic, light and refreshing. Just what it suggests: lyric.
(c) *The Spinto Voice.* Having both lyric and dramatic qualities and capacities and virtues and color potentials.
(d) *The Dramatic Voice.* Dark, powerful, rich, full-bodied, theatrical.

Thus, in theory at least, there might be such a thing as a colorature tenor, or a spinto bass, or a lyric contralto. In actual practice, however, not all applictions are made of the 6 times 4 = 24 possible sub-categories. Traditionally, some terms are dropped, and others are used.

The dramatic tenor is sometimes called a *tenore robusto* or *Heldentenor* (heroic tenor). A lyric bass might be called a *basso cantante*; a comic bass, a *basso buffo*; an especially deep and resonant bass, a *basso profundo*. A few rare voices are found in Russian cathedral choirs singing a full octave below the conventional basses. Astonishing voices, indeed, and the sound of these Russian basses is kind of like eggs frying on a hot pavement. They provide an edge to the regular bass sound much like a couple of string basses would in a normal choir.

To complete the picture of classical voices, two oddities must be mentioned, the countertenor and the castrato. Scholars are in disagreement as to whether the countertenor is a genuine unusually high male voice, or whether it is a male voice singing in falsetto, that is, singing with artificial sounds produced on only half of the vocal folds. Whatever it is, it is most assuredly a strange thing to see a full grown man sing in a voice which sounds very much like a high contralto. The total effect is a little unsettling, and countertenors are constantly having their manhood questioned, openly or in secret. Paul Esswood, married and the father of 2 sons, says, "People say things like 'women and countertenors first,' or, hearing the sound, ask solicitously, 'Is it anything physical?' "

With the castrato, it was indeed physical. From the 1500s through the 1700s and even into the 1800s the castration of young boy singers was a common practice in Europe, especially Italy. The relatively minor operation was performed before the boys reached puberty, so they grew into adulthood with the physical stature and strength of a man, but the vocal folds of a youth. This combination of adult male chest and lungs activating a pre-adolescent larnyx produced—according to historical accounts—a truly glorious sound. Castrati became superstars, often, and were much in demand for over 200 years. The last castrato died in 1928.

READING NOTES FOR CHAPTER TEN

[1]No effort will be made to distinguish between the singers who have died from those who are still alive and active. Through recordings, many singers long since gone are still part of the current musical environment—Jim Reeves, Louis Armstrong, Bing Crosby, Al Jolson, et al.

11

Choral Groups And Vocal Ensembles

The terms "vocal" and "choral" are used rather capriciously in the music world. Generally, the terms function much like the terms "chamber music" and "orchestral music" in the field of instrumental music. In chamber music, there would be (theoretically) only one player per part, while in orchestral music there would be several players performing the same part, say, Violin I.

In roughly the same way, the term vocal music would mean music for a small group, only one singer per part, like a vocal trio or a vocal quartet. And choral music would be music with many singers singing the same part, the Soprano I part, for

ILLUSTRATION: Church Choir. Courtesy of the Lakewood Baptist Church, Cincinnati.

example. The problem comes with a sextet or octet, though, where two singers might be singing the Soprano II part. The piece would probably called a vocal sextet, not a choral sextet.

Three large divisions can be made in this area, however, for all the confusion which exists: (a) large groups of mixed voices, men and women, (b) large groups of all men, or all women, and (c) special smaller groups, either mixed or uniformly male or female.

The Choir

As a generic term for the large group of mixed voices, male and female, the word *choir* is common. The conventional distribution of voices will be four—each of which is sometimes divided into first and second parts: Sopranos I and II, Altos (short for contraltos) I and II, Tenors I and II, and Basses I and II, with the "I's" taking the higher of two notes when the part is marked *divisi*. The music is called SATB music (for soprano, alto, tenor, and bass), and is the most common form of choral music by far. Most of the great choral music of Western Civilization has been cast in this setting.

Dozens of terms are found for the conventional SATB collection of voices, with the following loose distinctions:

Religious Groups. Usually called a choir. Seldom is the choral group at any local house of worship called a chorus. It is a choir. It may be Chancel Choir, or Motet Choir, or Sanctuary Choir, or Chapel Choir, or Temple Choir, or Adult Choir (to distinguish it from those guitar-strumming teenagers), or Service Choir, or Cathedral Choir, or whatever, but almost always "choir."

Educational Groups. High school and college groups may or may not be called a choir. The select group is often the *a cappella choir* (meaning, theoretically, that they would do their music without accompaniment). Other terms are Concert Choir, Mixed Chorus, Chorale, Concert Chorale, Chamber Choir, Chamber Chorus, or any mixture of the above.

Community and Professional Groups. The term Choral Union is used to denote a large community effort, as are the terms Choral Society, and Festival Chorus. Fred Waring had his "Pennsylvanians," although he called them a Glee Club for 20 years. Robert Shaw had his Chorale, as did Roger Wagner.

The Glee Club

As a generic term for a large group of men, or a large group of women, the term glee club is common. A men's glee club will have a four-way distribution of parts, Tenor I and II and Basses I and II, thus TTBB, and the "first tenor" (Tenor I) will usually have the melody.

A women's glee club will likewise have a four-way distribution of parts, Soprano I and II and Alto I and II, thus SSAA, and the "first soprano" will usually sing the melody (as she does in SATB Choir music, incidentally).

There are as many names for glee clubs as there ae imaginative glee club directors: The King's Men, The Queen City Belles, The Seattle Singers, the Manhattan Choraleers, as well as all the high school and college Buccaneers, Chordettes, Musical men, and Lyric Ladies. Anything goes as long as they wear the school colors.

Special Groups

One special group, the barbershop chorus, breaks tradition a little by the "voicing" of its four-way distribution. The melody lies in the voice second down from the top, "the lead" as he is called. Above him is the tenor. Immediately below him is the baritone, and on the bottom is the bass. The parts are simply called tenor, lead, baritone, and bass (and not designated TLBB, but designated, if anything, TTBB—for Tenor I and II and Bass I and II, but in the "barbershop style".

This barbershop style produces a special brilliance and ring to the chords which makes it a colorful musical experience, indeed. The whole barbershop flavor is much denigrated by musical sophisticates, and much loved by everyone else. Down-home male gospel quartets often voice their arrangements this way, too, and suffer the same musical criticism as a result.

Mixed gospel quartets will often follow the same voicing principle, with a female voice (usually a contralto) singing what would be the barbershop "lead." It produces that unique Sunday Morning TV Revival Hour sound which is surely as American as the hot dog.

Several other special groups bring joy to the hearts of the people, too. Madrigal Singers, Jazz-Rock Swingers, and others carry on in the high schools and colleges—each with a special repertory of songs which they do for their particular audiences. In the old days, there were a great many pop groups, like the Pied Pipers, the Modernaires, the Andrews Sisters, the Four Freshmen, the Hi-Lo's, and others. Later came the Beach Boys, the Beatles, the Supremes, and Crew Cuts, the Orioles, the Jackson Five, the Eagles, and hundreds of vocal groups.

A recent development in America is the "show choir." It is a select group, open by audition to the best 16-18 voices in the school or college. Show choirs often change costumes during their concerts, move around a lot in imaginative choreographed routines, and appear frequently as public relations goodwill agents on behalf of the music department. Show choirs have special arrangements which sometimes imitate big band voicings—with the female voices divided three ways (like the trumpet section of the big bands), and the male voices divided four ways (like the saxophone section). These show choirs draw their sociomusical inspiration from the theme-park reviews so common all over America—flashy, enthusiastic, up-beat, highly entertaining, and just a bit plastic.

All in all, the American musical environment has had its fair share of singers and singing groups, and it is still changing. There is no greater joy than singing with disciplined gusto, and it looks as though the rich variety and colorful diversity of America's choral groups and vocal ensembles is a permanent item on the aesthetic agenda for quite some time to come.

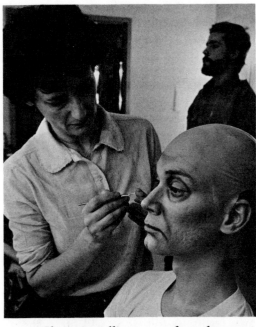

12

Small Secular Forms For Voices

Short (small) pieces of secular music for voices come in several varieties, and the textbook distinctions in this and the next three chapters are arbitrary distinctions, to be sure. Still, for study purposes, it is good to isolate the little non-religious musical operations from the big ones.

The terms are used a little loosely in the trade, but there is a general tendency to speak of *vocal forms* (also called *song forms*) to refer to music which will be sung by a solo singer (or a small group, at best), and to speak of *choral forms* to refer to music which will be sung by a fairly large group.

SOLOISTIC FORMS

Every known culture in every known historical period has had its body of songs for all occasions. Non-industralized societies practice an oral-aural song culture of astonishing depth, diversity, and utility. With the invention of the printing press and the subsequent emergence of what McLuhan calls a

ILLUSTRATION: Make-up preparations for an opera role. Courtesy of the CCM Publicity Office, Cincinnati, Ohio.

"visually oriented print culture," Western Civilization moved into an age of written song styles; but even today a large part of the song culture is predominantly oral-aural: country music, jazz, rock, folk, and a major portion of the pop music of the land is delivered and received—through tapes and discs—in a 20th Century "electronic global village" version of the ancient and traditional social process.

Whether secular or religious, three species of songs have arisen: the folk song out of peasant cultures, the pop song out of a commercial tradition, and the art song out of the classical tradition. These are theoretcal academic distinctions, of course, but useful as analytic tools.

(1) The *folk song* swells up out of a given society as a musical declaration of deep feelings about love, work, motherhood, sadness, loneliness, tribal achievements, and the like. In many cases the original composer is unknown, although an ancient singer probably cast the thing up in a cohesive statement sometime, somewhere. Modifications and mutations of both the text and the melody occur continuously from one generation to another, each generation revealing the underlying eternal truth in its own terms. A folk song will often show certain characteristic melodic contours and rhythmic figures which mark it clearly the product of a specific ethnologic origin—Spanish, Russian, Italian, Scandinavian, Anglo-Celtic, French, or whatever.

(2) The *pop song* is written for a specific show, act, consumer market, singer, recording date, publisher's request, or similar socioeconomic purpose. The composer is known, but more often the song is identified with the singer-performer who first brought the song into national visibility. A pop song may enter the folk repertory almost immediately, as did Irving Berlin's "God Bless America," sung by America's super-mom, Kate Smith, during the early days of World War II. Slight modifications and mutations of the melody of a pop song may appear through the years, but the text remains pretty constant. The pop song, like the authentic folk song, shows certain characteristic features which clearly mark it as the product of a given sub-culture. "Give My Regards to Broadway" (even excluding the text) simply could not have been conceived, musically, by Tex Ritter or Frank Zappa or Lawrence Welk.

(3) An *art song* is usually written for a specific potent text which has come to the attention of a classical composer. The text is often a famous, or at least a very high quality, poem by the composer's friend, and the composer makes an effort to match quality to quality. The result is a piece in which the accompaniment is interlaced with the melodic and poetic fabric of the text in such a way as to be inseparable thereafter. No one, for example, would dare perform an art song by Franz Schubert (*Der Erlkoenig*, say) with any other than the original piano accompaniment. The singer and pianist would be drummed out of the arts. The thing is cast up once and forever, and will go through no mutations or modifications as do folk and pop tunes.

Like folk and pop tunes, art songs reflect the culture of their origin, and occasionally, though less often than folk and pop tunes, find their way into the common musical property of the masses. The German Romantics brought the art song (the *Lied*, as it is called, in this case; plural = *Lieder*) to a peak of refinement and sophistication. Art songs are usually sung in the original language of their setting to preserve the total conception. Art song recitalists thus spend years perfecting their German, French, and Italian diction so they can do justice to the art song repertory. Russian is needed, too, but less often, since the choice of material is more limited and the market smaller and less demanding.

A special kind of pop song might be mentioned at this point, the so-called "commercial." Commercials are nothing new to humanity, and certainly did not originate with Tom Mix singing "Shredded Ralston for Your Breakfast" in the 1930s. Since the beginning of time, music has been used to set the mood for everything from war to religion to sex to selling fish in ancient Rome to selling flowers in London. The Jewish prophets had small bands of musicians with them when they roamed the countryside telling their story. All evidence indicates that the powerful emotional-subliminal effect of music was well known long before Coca-Cola taught the world to sing for the real thing.

The technique is being continuously refined, incidentally. The corporations Strohs, Pepsi, Coca-Cola, and others now have many versions of their basic jingle, each designed for different radio stations in different markets—a country version, a rock version, a jazz version, and a MOR version. The history of "commercials" and "theme songs" which go along with specific radio and TV shows would certainly be an interesting doctoral dissertation some day for an ambitious social psychologist.

Songs come in three species (folk, pop, and art), and also in three formal designs: (a) a one-time declaration, (b) a strophic narrative, and (c) a through-composed thread.

The One-Time Declaration

Just what it says. One bold, tight, highly integrated statement, like the Beatles' "Yesterday." No series of verses. No long and inolved story; just one quick poetic capsule. The tune may be one-part, or binary, or ternary in form, and will run probably around 32 measures in length. The 32-bar pop tune, eight measures each for an A-A-B-A kind of ternary design, was the classic model all through the early part of this century well into the 1960s.

There seems to be some experimentation, though, cerebral or intuitive, with the 32 bar standard. Roberta Flack's beautiful delivery of Ewan MacColl's "First Time Ever I Saw Your Face" breaks with the tradition quite dramatically. It has two opening sections of 17 measures each, then a final section of 28 measures. Burt Bacharach's "Raindrops Keep Fallin' On My Head" deviates, also, from the old standard 8-8-8-8 (A-A-B-A) design. "Raindrops"falls into sections of A-A-B-A, but the measure numbers are 9-9-10-12. Most unusual.

Dozens and dozens of the newer popular songs have broken out of the conventional mold ("Colour My world," with 13 measures, total; "Candy Man," with measure units of 14-14-10-14; and "What I Did for Love," with sections of 11-10½-8-15). The old standard 32 bar popular song has many new companions, these days.

The Strophic Narrative

Two kinds. The *single-unit* strophic narrative (*strophe* = Gr. "stanza"), and the *verse-refrain* strophic narrative.

(a) The single-unit package has the same music, over and over again, stanza after stanza, until the complete story has been told. "Tom Dooley," and "Amazin' Grace," and "Blowin' in the Wind." Economy of musical materials is the goal, here, and thus the single-unit strophic narrative is often in one-part, or else in binary form. Ternary form, with its contrasting center section (called, in the trade, the "bridge," or the "release," or the "channel"), would detract from the consistency and simplicity of the basic musical material, which, once presented, ought to recede in deference to the message of the unfolding stanzas of the text.

(b) The verse-refrain strophic narrative will, likewise, appear in Spartan simplicity and economy, but in a double package, with the refrain serving as a recurring interlude which throws the verses (stanzas) into bolder relief. Stephen Foster's "O Susanna" and hundreds of other camp and recreation songs owe their longevity to the psychic pleasures of the crowd joining in on the chorus (refrain) each time while the song leader runs through the many many verses, both traditional and newly invented right then and there.

The verse-refrain package is kind of a generous A-B design, with the A-text ever changing and the B-text ever constant. Both A and B musical materials are constant. Scholars find this call-and-response delivery all over the world in one form or another.

The Through-Composed Thread

Almost by definition, through-composed techniques give the art song its special status. Composed with fresh musical materials all through the several stanzas, the art song must be conceived and consumed as a total large-scale experience. The comfortable repetition of the folk and pop strophic narratives is precisely what the art song composer wants to avoid at all costs. There will be recurring fragments of familiar musical materials, perhaps, so the art song does not feel formless, but the composer is ever so careful to avoid repetition of any sizeable segments.

In the famous "Erlkoenig," for example, there are eight stanzas to Goethe's text, but Schubert has masterfully captured the changing nuances of each new stanza with new musical gestures to give increased psychoemotional depth and dramatic force to the story. The piano accompaniment is interwoven into the aesthetic matrix with such skill that the entire experience would be destroyed without that specific piano accompaniment. Nor would that piano accompaniment make sense without those specific words. The thing is a total fusion of text and music. Inseparable. That's what an art song is all about, and why it is held in such high esteem by classical composers and audiences.

SMALL GROUP CHORAL FORMS
A pop song may be sung by the entire group, the Bee Gees, for example, and yet remain, essentially, a "soloistic" musical conception, capable of being delivered by a solo singer, on occasion, without a great loss of musical intent. There are a few small-scale secular musical operations for voices which could not possibly be reduced for solo flight, however.

The Madrigal
Although there were madrigals in Italy in the 1300s and in the 1500s, and in England and other countries in the 1500s, it is usually only the English madrigal which gets sung much in the high schools and colleges. And those English madrigals sometimes come with names like "songs," and "sonets," and "canzonets," and "ayres," four, or five, or six "parts" to be sung by anywhere from 8 to 12 singers with plenty of sparkle and vitality.

The real fun of the madrigal is in the rhythmic interplay between parts.The tune goes bouncing along from altos to tenors to sopranos to basses with entrances two or three measures removed from each other in what musicians call imitative counterpoint. Throw a few fa-la-la-la's in here and there, and the thing is over in 6 minutes, perhaps. Today, as in

England in the 1500s, madrigals are light, good-natured, musical fun. Thomas Morley's "My Bonny Lass She Smileth" is a classic example of the madrigal at its best.

There was a slow, serious madrigal with beautifully inventive and colorful chordal texture, also, but this kind of madrigal is not so commonly done.

The Quodlibet

In the field of classical music, especially in the earlier days of the Renaissance and Baroque periods, composers sometimes had fun by combining well-known texts or musical quotations in a purposefully humorous mish-mash. C.P. E. Bach said that such tom-foolery was common in his family. Classical composers are a bit too serious about their art these days, and they seldom engage in such things, except for Peter Schickele.

The closest thing available today—and it would be a quodlibet in every sense of the original term—is the barbershop quartet comedy number in which tunes from all over creation come streaming in with and without their original texts. The Atomic Bums, a barbershop quartet out of Minneapolis in the 1940s, used to do a take-off on *Rigoletto* (the famous quartet scene) (by Verdi) tossing in the famous "Figaro, Figaro" theme (from Rossini's *Barber of Seville*) and other fragments from other operas by Puccini and friends. It was a hilarious quodlibet, and brought the house down every time.

The Broadway Rouser

Another kind of musical experience which would suffer terribly by being reduced to soloistic dimensions is the Broadway scene where a lot of singers get into the action. Something like "Officer Krupke" from Bernstein's *West Side Story*, for example, simply does not make sense as a vocal solo. Nor is it a genuine choir number. Many Broadway shows have scenes (musical numbers) which are neither full-blown choral items nor genuine solos. The term Broadway rouser will serve to identify this kind of vocal-choral music. Broadway veterans would probably refer to such musical selections as the "Officer Krupke number."

MISCELLANEOUS TITLES FOR VOCAL AND SMALL GROUP CHORAL MUSIC

As with instrumental music, there are a number of terms encountered rather frequently which need clarification.

Air (*Ayre*). Used over the centuries, essentially, for "song." When found in instrumental music, it will be a kind of "melody without words."

Aria. An elaborate solo song—existing alone, or more often, as part of an opera, or oratorio, or cantata.

Arietta. A short aria.

Arioso. Note quite a full-blown aria, but somewhere between an aria and a recitative.

Ballad. Several meanings earlier, but now, generally, a narrative told in simple popular-flavored musical terms.

Ballade and *Ballata* and *Balleto.* Special names for special historical forms. Seldom used today with any predictable distinct meaning.

Blues. 12-measure vocal bitter-sweet lamentations-celebrations on the Black Experience.

Cabaletta. A short operatic tune of pronounced popular style.

Canzona. Italian term for lyrical song.

Carol. A traditional hymn-like tune for Christmas (or, occasionally, Easter and the month of May).

Catch. Early name for what is now called a round.

Chanson. French term for song.

Descant. A special elaborate "countermelody" sung along with a traditional fairly simple melody.

Dirge. A song for a funeral or memorial service.

Ensalada. Spanish songs of humorous character.

Equale. A composition for all equal (all male or all female) voices.

Lied. German term for song, especially the "art song."

Medley. A collection of tunes, sung or played without interruption.

Psalm. A religious composition based on one of the texts in the Book of Psalms.

114

Recitative. The rapid delivery of many thoughts and narrative connections before the appearance of an aria.

Rota. Early name for *round.*

Round. Strict repetition, in different voices, of a fairly simple tune. "Row, Row, Row Your Boat," for example.

Serenata. A short secular cantata for the birthday of a member of the royalty.

Spiritual. An Afro-American song to God.

Vocalise. An extended melody sung on a single vowel, without text.

13

Large Secular Forms For Voices

One of the curious conditions of the field of music is the return of basic human desires in different social and historical settings.

SONG CYCLES AND CONCEPT ALBUMS

Around the early 1800s there developed among composers an urge to enlarge the song form, to give it a broader canvas for a longer emotional response. Beethoven's *An die ferne Geliebte* (1816) (*To the Distant Beloved*) on texts by Jeitteles seems to have inspired others to similar efforts. Schubert's *The Miller's Daughter* (1823) and *The Winter's Journey* (1827) are well known and often performed. Robert Schumann, Gustave Mahler, Vaughan Williams, Arnold Schoenberg, and many others wrote beautiful song cycles in which a sustained narrative thread was explored with great success.

ILLUSTRATION: Opera scene. Courtesy of the CCM Publicity Office, Cincinnati, Ohio.

In a similar manner, obeying the same urge, modern popular musicians have cast up large experiences in their concept albums. Paul McCartney said the Beatles were inspired to do *Sgt. Pepper* by Frank Zappa's *Freak Out* (1966). Later Bob Dylan did *John Wesley Harding* dealing with loners, outcasts, drifters, immigrants, and saints. Laura Nyro's *Eli and the Thirteenth Confession* (1968) traced a young girl's growth from childhood to adulthood. Willie Nelson produced an album called *Yesterday's Wine* following a man's life from birth to death.

If a story line is delivered in full costume, on stage, a new and exciting dimension becomes available, the theatrical experience.

OPERA

All through the ages, singers and instrumentalists have been drawn together in large scale theatrical affairs. In addition to religious celebrations (to be discussed later), there have always been non-religious occasions when the tribe felt the need to do something up in a big way: to begin a new season of the year, to commemorate an important historical event in the life of the community, to entertain their noble rulers, to sing the joys of having conquered an enemy, and so on.

The formalized ritual of an opera or Broadway show serves, on a plane once removed, the same purpose in modern society. The audience lives through the vicarious conflict-resolution-celebration experience with real emotions being generated in the admittedly artificial circumstances. And it is artificial, to be sure. In real life no one gets stabbed, then leans up against a post to sing a seven minute aria, "Thou hast stabbed me, Oh Villain."

But basketball is artificial, too. In real life, grown men seven feet tall simply do not run around knocking each other down in order to stuff a ball through a little wire rim. Detective stories are artificial, too. In real life, a typical male will go through his entire adult period without seeing one genuine murder or getting involved in one genuine fist fight.

The arts, and games, and the theater are all artificial. Musical productions have the added artificiality of a musical delivery of the circumstances of the drama, but the music adds to, rather than detracts from, the total effect, because music has the power to generate, and retrieve, emotions only vaguely experienced for real. It is all very complex and symbolic. So— (a) take the symbolic ritual for what it is, and (b) sit back and enjoy it.

History of Opera

(1) In its present form, opera goes back to the early 1600s when a group of Florentine writers, artists, and musicians tried to develop a new musico-theatrical form in imitation of what they thought ancient Greek dramatic productions had been. It is evident, now, that they missed the target; but they came up with "opera" (*opera* = plural for *opus*, meaning "work," thus *opera in musica* = works in music). The new musical stage productions caught on quickly, and several Italian schools of opera appeared in Venice, Rome, and Naples throughout the 1600s, and a little later in England, France, Germany, and Russia. This first period in the history of opera is often called the Early Baroque Period (1590-1680).

Stylistically these first operas were stiff and formalized. The characters lack emotional and theatrical contrasts so necessary for modern audiences. These operas are seldom performed today, therefore, except for an occasional presentation of Claudio Monteverdi's *Orfeo* (1607), a memorable work which stands head and shoulders above the others of this early period.

(2) The High Baroque period in the history of opera (1680-1760), sometimes called Neapolitan Opera, because Naples was the largest and most energetic center of activities, moved decidedly in the direction of more action, more emotional sweep, more musical and theatrical contrasts. Alessandro Scarlatti wrote over 100 operas in this style. Handel wrote 30 or so, his *Giulio Cesare*, 1724, being one of the few works from this entire historical period which is still performed today. By today's standards, these operas are still rather cold and formal, although one of the great melodies of all time comes fromt his period: the famous "Largo" (originally Larghetto), occurs at the beginning of Handel's *Xerxes* which

opened in London on April 15, 1738.

(3) A third historical period (1760-1850) cuts across Classic and Romantic aesthetic trends, from Mozart to Wagner. Opera as it is generally known today began to take shape, and it has not changed all that much since. C. W. Gluck's reforms brought a dramatic authenticity and tighter musical fabric to the art form. The singers had been destroying the overall theatrical and musical cloth of opera by their overbearing manner and their over-long improvisations and embellishments at every opportunity. Gluck and others began to change things in the middle of the century. Gluck's *Orfeo* (1762) stands out as an example of the new way, with accompanied reciatives (*accompagnato*), rather than so many (*secco* [dry]) recitatives; with the chorus and ballet both integrated more purposefully into the show.

From this third period comes one of the most famous of all operatic characters, Figaro. Beaumarchais created three stories about Figaro, and two of them were turned into opera masterpieces: *The Marriage of Figaro* (1786) by Mozart, and *The Barber of Seville* (1816) by Rossini. The third story, *The Culpable Mother*, has no operatic tradition.

(4) Romantic Opera (1850-1920) brings the art to many of its greatest and most memorable moments. Nearly all of the famous names and famous scenes held so dear by opera buffs (and spoofed so often by professional comedians) come from this Romantic Age. All of Europe was busy: the Italians Puccini, Verdi, Leoncavallo, and Mascagni; the Frenchmen Bizet, Gounod, and Massenet; the Russians Moussorgsky, Borodin, and Rimsky-Korsakov; and the overpowering productivity of the great German, Richard Wagner.

There are some interesting tendencies in these national schools. The Italians sought out the glorious sound of the human voice and presented it in brilliant simplicity and clarity against a relatively clear but highly colorful orchestral backdrop. The French composers took a bit more interest in drama and dancing, and the French operas are therefore a little more tightly laced together overall. The Russians worked with a large brush, and painted bold scenes in grandiose musical settings with large-scale pageantry everywhere in full detail. The

English left few works in the main category, but stole the show in light, witty, chamber-like operettas. The German genius will be treated separately under *music drama*, shortly.

(5) Modern Opera (1920-present) completes the story. Although there are some very traditional and some very modernistic works, no significant shift in the aesthetic thrust of the art form has emerged. One powerful work stands out early in the century, Alban Berg's *Wozzeck* (1925), a drama of great emotional intensity and musical depth.

In addition to some successful operas in a rather conventional style (Menotti's *Amahl and the Night Visitors* [1951], Britten's *Albert Herring* [1947], Floyd's *Susannah* [1955]), there have been several interesting experiments in jazz and rock, but no singular masterpiece has captured the fancy of America's opera crowd.

George Gerschwin's *Porgy and Bess* (1935) surely reached high in musical and dramatic gestures, and it still holds up year after year on stage. Some scholars call it America's one and only true operatic statement; others call it simply an unusually strong Broadway show. Leonard Bernstein has said that Broadway is, in fact, America's real opera, meaning, of course, that Broadway is the most uniquely American contribution to the musical stage traditions of Western Culture.

Some of the great stories which might have been made into operas in previous times have been made into blockbuster movies and TV docudramas—Watergate, Three Mile Island, Karen Silkwood, the Iranian Hostages, Neil Armstrong's Moon Walk, the Jonestown Mass Suicides. These are powerful events which future opera composers might tackle. Time will tell if the towering moments of modern history will ever become opera plots. There seems to be a tendency—today, as in previous days—to allow a little historical distance before working up potent stories into operatic material.

Opera Categories

Operas come in two main categories and several sub-categories. The distinctions are not always pure, and the categories overlap somewhat, of course.

(1) *Opera seria* meant, originally, an opera in which everything is sung throughout. No spoken dialogue anywhere in the work. A large production, with full orchestral accompaniment, on a big serious topic. *Aida* (1871) by Giuseppe Verdi (1813-1901) and *Carmen* (1875) by Georges Bizet (1838-1875), sometimes called "grand" operas, are typical of this first main category.

A special kind of *opera seria*, developed by Richard Wagner (1813-1883), came to be known as *music drama*. Wagner wrote the text and music, invented new instruments to get the sounds he wanted, gave elaborate instructions for everything from scenery design to the acoustical properties of the stage area. He wrote the original story, himself. He came up with an all-inclusive total art work (*Gesamtkunstwerk*, as the Germans say), in which all artistic components are interlaced in one massive continuously unfolding and developing psycho-aesthetic experience.

Vocal solos weave in and out of Wagner's musical fabric-at-large; *leitmotifs* (leading motives) identify most major characters, objects, and emotions throughout the stories; and all this grows out of what is essentially an orchestral concept. The whole offering has been called, fittingly, "symphonic opera." *Tristan and Isolde* (1865) is an excellent example.

(2) *Opera comique* meant, originally, an opera which permitted some passages of spoken dialogue, often humorous, but not necessarily so. "Comic opera" grew up as little diversions performed during the intermissions between the three big acts of *opera seria*. Spoken dialogue, popular tunes, and humorous scenes provided just the right kind of relief from the heavy substance and tone of the *opera seria*. Before long, the little comic operas moved out on their own. The growing middle classes rather enjoyed the light-hearted fun of comic opera: Germany developed its *Singspiel*, Italy the *opera buffa*, England the *ballad opera*, and France the *opera comique* (from whence comes the generic term for the whole category).

In addition to the above, two later developments in the general area of *opera comique* have dominated the field for quite some time now—the European form called *operetta* and the American form called the Broadway musical.

An *operetta* is just what the term suggests, a "little opera." The "little" aspect refers to the tone and weight of the music and the plot, not to the length of the work. The normal-in-length but light and humorous works of W. S. Gilbert (librettist 1836-1911) and Arthur Sullivan (composer 1824-1900), for example, are called operettas. The short-in-length but serious *Pagliacci* (text and music by Ruggeiro Leoncavallo [1858-1919]), however, is never called an operetta.

A special brand of American opera comique, the Broadway show, has captured the fancy of theater goers all over the world. For most folks, a Broadway show is a Broadway show, but insiders sometimes draw a distinction between a musical play, also called a book musical (strong plot laced together with equally strong music and dancing), *Oklahoma*, for example, and a musical comedy (thin plot puffed up with loosely connected tunes, girls in abundance, and comedy routines), *Gentlemen Prefer Blondes*, for instance.

COMMON INGREDIENTS IN MUSICAL SHOWS

Some fairly predictable things happen in all musico-theatrical productions, whether a powerful grand opera or a light musical comedy.

The overture by the orchestra sets the tone and mood of the occasion, sometimes offering a snatch of the more prominent melodies to come later in the show, sometimes just setting the mood for the opening scene, sometimes capturing the spirit of the entire show to come in a generalized way. If it is really good, an operatic overture might outlive the show itself and linger in the concert orchestra repertory long after the opera has been forgotten. Gioacchino Rossini's (1792-1868) overture to the opera *William Tell* (1829), for example, still pleases concert goers season after season (along with Lone Ranger fans).

The big moments in any musical show are the solos by the leading stars. Called *arias* in opera, and simply vocal solos in Broadway, these full-blown musical statements give the show its most memorable moments. All dramatic and narrative elements are suspended, briefly, while the main character sings a beautiful song. If the area is done exceptionally well, the whole show stops cold while the audience bursts forth in exuberant "Bravos!" (for a male singer) or "Bravas!" (for a female singer).

An aria is often preceded by a *recitative*, a "recitation" of the circumstances which have led the singer to the point where the emotional circumstances seem to demand a full song-like treatment. The recitative is, of course, less melodic, less musically spun-out, less artistically developed. It is really a preparation for the aria. In a Broadway show, the verse to the tune serves the same function as the recitative to the aria. If the Broadway tune has no verse (more and more common, these days), a few spoken lines will lead comfortably into the tune.

Every good show has a couple of big chorus numbers. At this time the stage is full of singers in a grand spectacular. In opera, the most famous of these big numbers is the grand finale of Act II in Giuseppe Verdi's *Aida* (1871), complete with animals from the local zoo for the Triumphal March. This is show biz at its highest, and never fails to please the audience.

Many shows have dance scenes during which a troupe of dancers will somehow find their way into the show, often on rather flimsy narrative needs. Some excuse if found or manufactured, and the dancers appear from the wings to delight the audience and to provide the show with some psychological breather space. The better the show, the more believable is the dance sequence, and the more it makes a genuine contribution to the growth of the show. Weaker shows simply bring on the dancers. In any event, after the dance sequence, the show picks up again, and everyone is ready for more pure music.

Every show will have a love duet between the leading lady and the leading man, a soprano and a tenor (in opera) or the two leading voices (possibly a baritone and mezzo-soprano, in Broadway). It may or may not be terribly convincing as a love scene, but it is often the most beautiful musical event in the show. Most shows have several small vocal ensembles (trio, quartet, quintet), also. These are very special moments in a musical show. In no other art form can the same thing occur— four or five brilliant singers each delivering a specific interpretation of the current state of emotional entanglements in the plot, all interlaced with orchestral colors. A truly unique artistic offering. The quartet scene from Verdi's *Rigoletto* (1851), for example.

All in all, the essential musical and theatrical features are much the same in opera, operetta, Broadway, and all the various hues and shades between and among. The tone and substance of the stories are different, and the style and technique of the music are different, of course. Opera is "classical" music; Broadway is "popular" music. Opera tackles grandiloquent themes; Broadway seeks out more common concerns. Opera is high brow. Broadway is middle-brow. But the basic human condition being served is identical—the pure joy of getting involved in an interesting story and having it all worked out before you in appealing music by colorful singing actors. A feast for eyes and ears. Fun.

THE ARMY OF TALENT

Broadway shows, operettas, comic operas, musical plays, serious operas, music dramas—musical stage productions by whatever name—are frightfully expensive to mount because of the enormous costs of lighting equipment, scenery construction, theater space, paint, canvas, and rope, yes, but also because of the large number of high-powered professionals needed to bring a big show into reality.

In no particular order of importance, because a good show needs everyone at the peak of talent, here is an idea of who's who and does what in a musical show.

The author of the novel, or play, is the beginning of the thing, of course. Often a novel is made into a straight drama then made into a musical show. Good stories surface nearly every generation. In opera, some effort has been made, recently, to choose more modern themes in an effort to capture new audiences. John Steinbeck's *Of Mice and Men* was made into an opera by Carlisle Floyd, a few years ago, with good results according to the music critics.

A librettist (opera) or lyricist (Broadway) converts the story into a text which readily lends itself to being set musically. The composer then takes the text, and does just that. When a composer and lyricist really click, they often continue on for several productions. Richard Rodgers (composer) and Oscar

Hammerstein, II (lyricist) became a near industry with *Oklahoma* (1943), *State Fair* (1945) a movie, *Carousel* (1945), *Allegro* (1947), *South Pacific* (1949), *The King and I* (1951), *Me and Juliet* (1953), *Pipe Dream* (1955), *The Flower Drum Song*, (1958), and *The Sound of Music* (1959).

A different team—Wolfgang Mozart (composer) and Lorenzo da Ponte (librettist)—wrote three masterpieces together, *The Marriage of Figaro* (1786), *Don Giovanni* (1787), and *Cosi Fan Tutte* (1790).

The producer raises the money to get the show started. He may or may not take an active role in the working details of the show, but rather often he does. David Merrick and David Susskind have good track records as producers of both musical and legitimate theater works in New York. Until recently, Rudolph Bing, of the Metropolitan Opera Company, was the world's foremost opera producer.

The director is the chief working-details executive. Kind of like a baseball manager. It is really his show, even though he probably gets a lot of advice from above, and a lot of noise from below. His job is just about as secure as a baseball manager's job, also. Things better keep looking up.

The star singers in the lead roles, and the would-be star singers in the secondary roles, get their jobs through audition in front of the director. The producer may well be there, too, along with some major sources of money. Established names may not have to really audition, but merely demonstrate that they are truly interested in the role. In opera, certain singers get known for doing an exceptional job in certain roles, and are simply hired for that role, sometimes years in advance.

The musical director makes all major musical decisions, beginning with the selection of a conductor, the hiring of the musicians, the choice of a rehearsal pianist, etc.

The conductor is the person who will actually stand in front of the orchestra with the baton in his hand. Quite often the musical director does his own conducting, but he may choose to give the job to an assistant or colleague.

The musical arranger will take the composer's brief sketches (probably only a melody line, words, and chords) and make a full musical score. This "arrangement" may be rather sparse, also, consisting of the overall sweep of the idea, with the specific note-for-note manuscript prepared by round-the-clock copyists. Robert Russell Bennett, a very successful arranger of Broadway musicals, would sketch out his plan for the score, but only with enough information so that the copyists could carry out their job—never with every single note written down. He was simply too busy, often working on three or four major productions at the same time.

The chorus master and vocal coach handle the training and guidance of the singers. Really big stars do not get coached much, of course.

The choreographer conceives the dance routines and teaches them to the dancers. Bob Fosse and Tommy Tune are two recent big names in the field of Broadway choreography. Agnes de Mille, a classical choreographer, did the dance routines for *Oklahoma*, with great success.

The set designer sketches out the total scenery, props, and all in complete detail so the master carpenter and his crew can construct exactly what is needed. Good opera sets, once constructed, get loaned around the country from one theater to another. After a few years, when an opera set has been bumped around quite a bit, some wealthy patron will commission a new set by a favorite set designer. There is some of this kind of trading around in Broadway musicals, but less than in opera.

A good set must be properly and imaginatively lighted by the lighting director, a creative artist type, who works very closely with the master electrician, a skilled craftsman type.

There may be a drama coach if the production needs some heavy-weight guidance in this area. There may be a musical consultant and historical consultant if the thing gets into a historical period very deeply.

There is always a costume designer who conceives the costumes in full detail so head seamstress and crew can make everything precisely as sketched out. Good costumes get loaned all around the country, too, like good sets. Costumes are usually made with plenty of extra material to allow for different body proportions. Costumes also have to be altered each time for the dozens of "supers" (short for supernumeraries = players without singing or speaking parts).

Add to this musical and theatrical army another whole army of promotion, sales, management, and transportation specialists, not to mention publishers' agents, copyright lawyers, recording contract negotiators, union representatives from all over the town, and the show gets pretty big, indeed.

Put them all together, they spell financial trouble for opera and Broadway all the time. Opera companies all over the world are subsidized by governments, wealthy patrons, and philanthropic foundations. Broadway makes it on the basis of a monster hit, like *My Fair Lady*, for example, which grosses in the millions, enough to sustain everyone through the next half-dozen much more modest shows.

MISCELLANEOUS THINGS

Several forms have been on the American scene at one time or another. Most of them belong to the "collection principle" of organizing a large-scale musical experience. Most of them also contained generous portions of non-musical fare interlaced between and among the musical happenings. The musical moments were, and are, however, the glue which holds the entire entertainment package together, and these musical moments are the memories which linger long in the minds of the audiences who found joy in the evening's entertainment.

The *minstrel show* derives from English music hall variety shows. The Irish buffoon was a standard item in English variety entertainment, and in the transfer got switched to the stereotyped blackface, "Mr. Bones." The minstrel show is a terrible chapter in America's history of race relations, but its contribution to musical theater was substantial from the 1840s into the early 1900s.

A minstrel show's first section would consist of a Grand Entrance of the whole crowd in ill fitting swallow-tail tuxedos, all in blackface except the middle man, Mr. Interlocutor. The entire first section was a string of vocal solos, virtuoso instrumental numbers, duets, trios, and such, all interspersed with frequent quips between and among Mr. Interlocutor, Mr. Bones (on one end), and Mr. Tambo (on the opposite end).

The second section, sometimes called the Olio, was a couple of short satire sketches or parody skits on popular social or political topics of the day. The whole thing concluded with a General Ruckus or Walk-Around. It was a delightful entertainment package, even though it feels ugly and cruel in the light of today's improved ethnic and racial awareness and respect.

Vaudeville had its roots in English beerhall entertainment. In America, this kind of variety show was cleaned up by the time Tony Pastor opened his Opera House in the Bowery section of New York in 1865. Soon "variety houses," that is, vaudeville theaters, sprang up all over America where the greatest names played—Harrigan and Hart, Lillian Russell, Weber and Fields, and hundreds of others. Keith, Albee, and Shubert Theaters appeared in every major metropolitan market in America.

There is no such thing anymore. Talking pictures forced the vaudeville houses to change from two performances per day to continuous entertainment of movies and vaudeville programs alternating throughout the better part of each day and evening. Radio finally pushed vaudeville out of the entertainment industry completely. Strangely enough, vaudeville came back in an electronic version in the great days of Ed Sullivan—dog acts, jugglers, comedians, magicians, singers, strong men, and anything else to capture the interest and delight the senses of the vast audience always hungry for the pleasures of variety entertainment.

Burlesque shows in the original were not strip-tease affairs, at all. That came later. Burlesque (from *burla*, meaning "joke") was a form of theater specializing in satirical skits and outrageous parodies designed to entertain the audience by revealing the frailties and imperfections of the human condition. The skits would be separated by singers and dancers and other novelty acts. As the movies and radio drew audiences away from live theater, the singing and dancing got more raunchy until the whole art form turned into a string of strippers.

The original idea of burlesque is still around, though, in the recent Carol Burnett successful TV series, in *Saturday Night Live*, and in Mel Brooks' movies. TV's "sit-coms" (situation comedies) are often burlesque treatments of normal human relationships, *The Jeffersons*, for example, and the *I Love Lucy* reruns.

Extravaganzas, as they were called in the late 1800s, came from a mixture of music, dancing, and a story. The story might be rather thin, but it was there. One of the first extravaganzas, *The Black Crook* (1866), caused quite a stir on the Eastern Seaboard because of its scantily clad dancers and its spectacular stage effects (a demon ritual, a hurricane in the mountains, a carnival, and March of the Amazons). The show was considered to be the work of the devil, and it was denounced with vigor by all respectable journalists, preachers, and politicians. Ticket sales soared after each criticism. The show ran for sixteen months and enjoyed many revivals.

Rock concerts are a kind of opera experience for American adolescents. The audiences at a rock concert are younger and dressed in a different manner, of course, from an opera audience, but several things are similar—the stunning pageantry of what transpires on the stage, the act of being seen by friends and acquaintances at the event, the firming up of self identity views by going to the event, the thought of making informal contact with certain people for future social or financial associations, and all the other normal reasons why people go to something special as they bring variety into their lives.

ILLUSTRATION: The Eagles in the early 1980's. Courtesy of Asylum Records.

Colorful and exciting as they are, rock concerts do not seem to be leading to a new art form.

The new art form, if there is one, and it is beginning to look like there really is, is Music Video. Two basic approaches have crystallized: (a) the concert clip, and (b) the concept piece. The concert clip shows various shots from different angles of the band on stage. The concept piece tells some kind of story, revealing the essential topic of the song in a mini-movie kind of display, or in abstract geometric symbols which try to capture the spirit of the song and its text. Music Video even has its own cable TV station, MTV (Music Television), which plays these videos 24 hours a day.

The popular music industry looks suddenly alive and eager for new talent, now that Music Video has arrived on the scene. Time will tell.

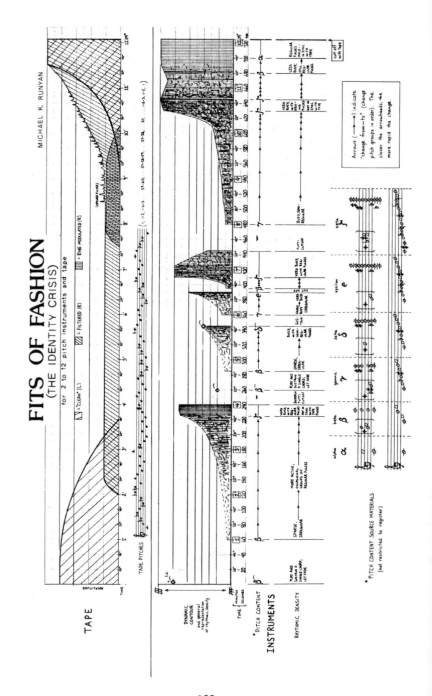

FITS OF FASHION
(THE IDENTITY CRISIS)
for 2 to 12 pitch instruments and tape

MICHAEL K. RUNYAN

Small Sacred
Forms
For Voices

The earliest small-scale religious musical utterances of any formalized design in Western Culture were probably from the book of *Psalms*. These little two-part verses, with contrasting or parallel sections, seem to have been rendered in what has become known as chant, or plainchant, and later Gregorian Chant (after Pope Gregory who tried to codify a large body of the music). Early psalms were often chanted on a single note, with a beginning and ending formula called a psalm tone. The very human inclination to embellish or decorate the delivery a bit has led to elaborate modifications and multi-voiced setting of later psalms.

A *hymn* is a poem of praise or adoration set to music. The term has been used since the beginning of time, it seems. The conventional characteristics of a hymn, today, are these: it will be sacred; it will be rather simple; it will be strophic, most likely;will be intended for congregational singing, rather than for a trained choral group. A gospel hymn will have that special down-home country flavor to it ("Amazin' Grace," for example) as opposed to the traditional run ("A Mighty Fortress is Our God").

OPPOSITE ILLUSTRATION: An example of modern musical notation by American composer, Michael K. Runyan. Copyright © 1982. All rights reserved. Used by permission.

133

A hymn arrangement will be sung by a trained group, and will be more involved in technical and musical modifications of the basic hymn tune. New words may be added, new musical interludes and new sections created, and the whole thing will emerge as a full-blown presentation by the choir.

The term *chorale* has a confusing history. The word choral (pronounced CORal) is an adjective meaning having to do with choirs. Choral music is music for choirs. The word choral (pronounced coRAL) means hymn. The spelling chorale (pronounced coRAL) has come into use for this second meaning. It is a useful spelling because it permits a distinction between *choral* music (anything for choir) and *chorale* music (something based on a chorale, that is, something based on a hymn).

Like other hymns, the chorale (German) will be strophic, simple, sacred, meant for the congregation to sing. Martin Luther was always on the look out for good pop tunes that he could convert to chorales, and tradition has it that Luther once said, "Why should the Devil have all the good tunes?"

The term *motet* has been around for 700 years or so now, and has meant many things at different times. It comes from *mot* = French for "word," and was first used to designate a part of the music to which words were being added. Over the many years, though, the term has come to mean, generally, a piece of music (a) for choir, not for congregation, (b) fairly complex, with contrapuntal passages in it, (c) often in Latin, (d) sacred, (e) unaccompanied, that is *a cappella*, and (f) medium length, like 6-9 minutes long.

The *anthem* is the Protestant version of the above, often Catholic, motet. All conditions are the same, with the exception that the anthem will be in English and will have an organ or piano accompaniment. A gospel anthem will be a fairly elaborate treatment of a fairly simple gospel tune. Another term for gospel anthem is Evangelical anthem. Everyone has heard this kind of thing on the Billy Graham Crusade with Cliff Barrows leading the choir through an elaborate arrangement of "How Great Thou Art."

A *spiritual* is that special black utterance to God. It is a magnificent cultural mix of African spirituality with Christian doctrine and European melodic materials and harmonies.

Religious pop tunes have always been around, also. Things like "He Touched Me" and "The King is Coming" have become standard items in Protestant worship services.

Several short religious vocal-choral works are encountered over and over again, and, by virtue of the derivation of the text, are likely to share certain general musical characterisics: (a) for trained singers, (b) in Latin, (c) complex and elaborate, (d) 8-10 minutes in length. These works come out of ten centuries of musico-religious productivity, so the above generalizations must be very liberally interpreted.

Adoramus te Christe. "We adore Thee, Christ" has been set to music hundreds of times by major composers every generation since the late Middle Ages. Likewise with *Ave Maria* ("Hail Thee, Mary") and with *Alleluia* ("Praise Ye the Lord").

A *magnificat* is a setting of the canticle of the Virgin, *Magnificent anima mea dominum* ("My soul doth magnify the Lord"), and has been treated by many major composers. Also *Te deum laudamus* ("We praise Thee, O God"), by, for example, Purcell, Handel, Berioz, Bruckner, Dvorak, Verdi, and many others.

Stabat mater dolorosa, from a 13th century text ("There stood the Mother") has been done by Josquin, Palestrina, Scarlatti, Pergolese, Haydn, Schubert, Rossini, Verdi, Dvorak, and others.

From a simple gospel hymn to an elaborate Te deum, composers are driven to declare themselves in songful praise to their Judaic-Christian God. The Jews and the Christians may disagree on some details, but they do agree on the monotheistic concept itself. It is this concept which has generated a large body of music in Western Culture.

15

Large Sacred Forms For Voices

THE MASS

Music and religious worship are intertwined in all cultures. In Western Civilization, the developments get very complex and sophisticated in the Late Middle Ages when composers began to take a hand in specific portions of the Mass, that is, the order of worship for the Catholic Church.

The Mass accumulated over the long history of the Church, retaining bits and pieces of Hebrew and Greek prayers and influences. By the early Renaissance, it had crystallized into an order of events in a rather strict outline (see next page). The Mass is nothing less than a complete re-enactment of the Last Supper, each and every time it is performed. A Low Mass will involve only the priest, and no parts will be sung. A High Mass will have the choir parts sung. A Solemn High Mass will use priest, deacon, and subdeacon, and all choir parts will be sung.

ILLUSTRATION: The Cincinnati May Festival Chorus and Orchestra. Courtesy of the Cincinnati Enquirer.

STRUCTURE OF THE MASS

ORDINARY ITEMS		PROPER ITEMS	
(A) Choir or Congregation	(B) Priest	(C) Choir or Congregation	(D) Priest
(2) Kyrie		(1) Introit	(4) Collect Prayer
(3) Gloria			(5) Epistle Reading (or Old Testament)
(9) Credo		(6) Gradual	
		(7) Alleluia (or Tract) Sequence	(8) Gospel Reading
		(10) Offertory Antiphon	
	(11) Offertory Prayers		(12) Secret Prayer
			(13) Preface
(14) Sanctus Benedictus	(15) Canon (Consecration)		
	(16) Pater Noster		
(17) Agnus Dei		(18) Communion Antiphon	(19) Postcommunion Prayer
	(20) Ite Missa Est*		

*Ite Missa Est would probably be translated "Go, this is the dismissal." However, the word *missa* came to be understood by some folks not as expressing the verbal notion of dismissal, but, rather, as a noun referring to the entire ceremony that had just taken place. Hence, "Go, this is the 'Mass.'" The term *mass* may derive from these circumstances.

Columns A and B, "Ordinary Items," stay the same day after day, Sunday after Sunday. Columns C and D, "Proper Items," change with the particular Sunday, Saint's Feast, or time of the Church Year.

If all this seems confusing, it is. In music appreciation studies, the important thing to notice is that Column A consists of Ordinary Items (constant) which would be sung occasionally (at the higher Masses) by a trained choir. When a composer set out to compose music for the Mass, then, his major efforts would go into the five items in Column A: Kyrie, Gloria, Credo, Sanctus and Benedictus, and Agnus Dei.

Up through the Renaissance, any Mass composed by a professional composer was probably intended, and could be used, for the actual worship service. As the Baroque Period progressed, though, the Masses got too elaborate for actual use in the worship service, and before long the Mass became, for all practical purposes, a concert piece, and a big one. Johann Sebastian Bach's *Mass in B-minor*, for example, would simply be out of place on a Sunday morning, with its need for full orchestra, soloists, large chorus, and all. A Mass by Palestrina, however, was written for a small *a cappella* choir, and would be quite appropriate for a Sunday morning.

In addition to the regular Mass, described above, there is a special Mass, the Requiem Mass, called such because it begins with the Introit *Requiem aeternam dona eis Domine* ("Give them eternal rest, O Lord"). As might be expected in a Requiem Mass, certain joyful portions are omitted (the Gloria and the Credo); the Alleluia is replaced by the Tractus; and a well-known sequence *Dies irae* ("Day of Wrath") is inserted. A *Requiem Mass* is performed to observe the death of an important member of the parish or some significant figure in Church history, and performed on All Saints Day.

Two other Masses exist: the Votive Mass (performed at the priest's request), and the Nuptial Mass (performed at Weddings). Neither of these forms has any history of special music having been written for it.

ORATARIO

An oratorio is a large-scale musical narrative by soloists, chorus, and orchestra. Biblical texts are most common, although a few grandiose secular oratorios are around. The oratorio has all the ingredients of an opera—that is, a story line, arias, duets, trios, choruses, instrumental interludes, an overture, etc.—but does not have opera's staging, scenery, dancing, or person-to-person dialogue. The oratario is like a massive biblical concert opera delivered in the third person without any staging devices.

The term oratorio comes from the middle of the 1500s when a special kind of pop-flavored religious order was founded by Filippo Neri. The religious services consisted of scripture readings, a sermon, and singing by different costumed singers representing God/Soul and Heaven/Hell. The group was known as the *oratoriani*, and had a building called the "oratorio" (oratory or chapel).

Out of these little allegorical presentations came the oratorio as it is known today, after many intermediate historical developments, of course. The model was readily available, though, by the time Bach and Handel began their work. Bach and Handel, especially Handel, gave the form a big historical moment with the middle classes; oratorios have been prominent in Christian affairs during Christmas and Easter ever since.

Oratorios come in two categories: (a) just plain oratorio, like Handel's famous *Messiah*, or Mendelssohn's *Elijah*, and (b) the Passion, an oratorio setting of the text of the Passion *Passio Domini nostri Jesu Christi*), from one of the Evangelists. A Passion, then, is the story of the suffering and death of Jesus of Nazareth in full oratorio dress.

CANTATA

For all practical purposes, a cantata is a baby oratorio, shorter and less involved, perhaps, but essentially the same kind of musical operation. The term comes from *cantare* = "to sing." Many historical styles and forms of both sacred and secular cantatas have come and gone. The form is now still quite popular with religious groups who are presenting some very formal "classical" cantatas, and also many less formal "popular" cantatas.

An oratorio will be anywhere from 50 to 150 minutes long. A cantata seldom runs more than an hour. An oratorio will often have large choruses, a double chorus, sometimes, with a full orchestra, and arias and small ensembles of considerable technical difficulty. Cantatas are less ambitious, generally, in every direction.

Of the nearly 300 cantatas written by J. S. Bach, only 190+ remain. Of these, several have become standard items in the repertory of the larger churches in Occidental Culture. *Christ lag in Todesbanden* ("Christ Lay in the Bonds of Death") is justly considered one of the best ever.

NEW DEVELOPMENTS

The cantatas of Dallas Holm, Otis Skillings, John Peterson, and others are essentially pop music with a religious text. They represent a trend, perhaps, in the direction of an important change in church music today.

Religious leaders are concerned about keeping their adolescents interested in the faith, and have thus permitted such things as a Jazz Mass, a Folk Mass, a Folk Cantata, and Rock Cantata, Jazz-Rock Services, and many other explorations into hitherto forbidden territory. Guitar-strumming youngsters—hair, beads, and all—are now singing out for Christ with the complete (well, almost complete) support of the elders and deacons.

Marriage ceremonies went through a period of some unusual developments, with jazz and rock and folk musicians delivering unorthodox statements in the midst of a ceremony written by the bride and groom themselves. The 1980s seem to be moving back toward more traditional things, however.

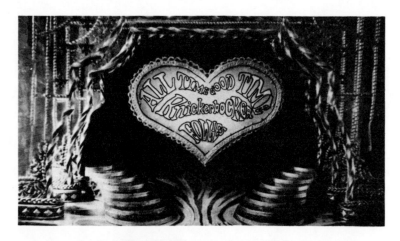

ALL-TIME GOOD-TIME KNICKERBOCKER FOLLIES

A review tracing the history of the American Musical Theatre. Produced by the Empire State Institute for the Performing Arts (of the State University of New York) Albany, N.Y.

Directed by Patricia Birch. Book by Hugh Wheeler. Scenic Design by R. Finkelstein. Music Supervision, George Harris and Joe Raposo.

Photo 1: Scenic Design Model. Photo 2: Scrim backdrops and painted floor used in the production. The scrim designs are based on actual programs, hand bills, and elements of sheet music cover illustrations. Used by permission of Richard Finkelstein.

142

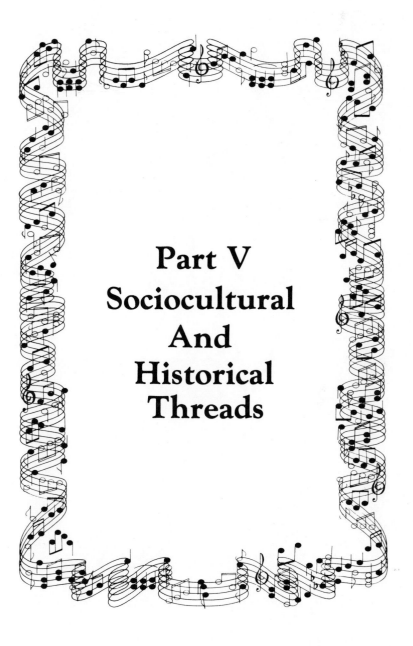

**Part V
Sociocultural
And
Historical
Threads**

16

A Theoretical Study Model

Music is a form of behavior. It does not exist separate from the human experience, as does, say, the law of gravity. Music derives from and reflects the people who create it. Like language, kinship patterns, political systems, sports activities, and all the other social rituals, music grows out of, and in turn reinforces, the accepted attitudes and cherished values of the cultural matrix of its origin.

To examine different kinds of music, then, requires an analytic tool which will slice through the surface elements, and expose the deeper tissues of the life style of the folks who have produced and are consuming the music. That is, a Cultural Frame of Reference is needed.

I. Cultural Frame of Reference.

A. Sociological Roots. What kind of people, from where, create the music? What special ethnic and cultural traits are evident? How strong are these socio-anthropological characteristics? What changes have occurred? What changes seem likely to come?

B. Psychoemotional Bases. Given their unique cultural characteristics, what are the peculiar and special attitudes toward life held in common by these particular people? What are their feelings above love, truth, beauty, God, fear, pain, time, space, loneliness, joy, sex, male and female roles, and all the other things in what Edward T. Hall, anthropologist, calls the "vocabulary of a culture?"

C. Musical Results. What kind of melodies, harmonies, rhythms, instrumental combinations, forms, musical gestures, sound patterns, and what kind of collective sociomusical rituals do these folks go through to celebrate and reaffirm the attitudes they hold in common? How does the specific musical language sustain and support the sociocultural attitudes? How is the musical language different from the musical language of other communities in Judaic-Christian Culture?

D. Topics of Concern. What specific issues are found over and over again in the songs and shows of the genre (jazz, or classical, or Broadway, or rock, or country music)? What traits are revealed in the messages between the lines? What topics are unique to this crowd? How does this particular community handle topics which they share in common with other communities?

Once the sociocultural terrain has been surveyed, the music of a given crowd will reveal itself in vivid clarity. The next step, then, is to trace the growth and development of the music since it first began to assume its currently recognizable character. That is, to set the music up in a position for an historical review.

One of the curious things about the major musical genres in America—classical, jazz, rock, Broadway, and country music—is that they have strikingly similar development patterns. It is possible, for example, to find in each a Classic Period followed by a Romantic Period followed by a Period of Experimentation. The "periods" are artificial and contrived, of course, as are all intellectual distinctions which deal with human behavior. Johann Sebastian Bach did not think of himself as a Baroque Composer, nor did Benny Goodman tell his band to play Classic Swing. These categories are historical fiction created to bring order to a mass of otherwise cumbersome details. Academicians do this all the time. They must. There simply is no other way to handle large bodies of information, especially in the humanities and social sciences.

Here, then, in blazing oversimplification of highly complex developments are some consistent "historical periods" through which each of the major musical genres in America has come:

II. Historical Review.

A. The Birth of the Genre. What were the circumstances of the formation of this particular kind of music (jazz, or classical, or Broadway, or country, or rock) as it began to emerge in its distinct individuality? When, where, and by whom does the music get lifted up to a position of historical visibility?

B. A Baroque Era. The term comes from traditional art history, and means a corruption of the previous original purity. During the Baroque Period of the various musical genres the major components and principles solidify, and the music assumes its essential substance and spirit. It is a period of bold declarations and colorful musical gestures which clearly fortell of more to come—even though these Baroque techniques and activities are fully and completely rewarding as musical experiences themselves.

C. A Classical Period. A time of settling down into a judicious balance of form and content; a time of clarity, precision, symmetry, restraint, and carefully controlled yet warm and lyrical statements. A time against which other times seem somehow more flamboyant and emotional.

D. A Romantic Period. A breaking out of the bonds of intellectual control and refinement. A time of sweeping gestures derived from unbridled feelings. The heart knows what the mind can never comprehend. As Goethe said, "All the knowledge I possess everyone else can acquire, but my heart is all my own."

E. A Modern Period. A turning away from the unbuttoned exhibitionism of the Romantics. A time of wide experimentation and self-searching. A time of strong and contrasting thrusts—greater intellectualization of the music, on one hand, and a powerful return to emotional roots, on the other hand.

All this is entertaining and interesting—and highly debatable. Is Beethoven a Classic or a Romantic composer? Did the Beatles create a Classic Period or a Romantic Period in the history of rock? Is *Oklahoma* one of the great Classic moments in Broadway or one of the great Romantic moments? Each professor and each student will have a different view, perhaps.

Good. The purpose of education is not to deliver a bundle of preconceived answers. The purpose of education is, and ought to be, to give students the tools for preparing their own informed opinion on things—especially in the humanities where opinions on the meaning of facts (answers) are as important as the facts themselves.

For all its limitations and imperfections—because the whole scheme is a grand experiment—here follow five chapters treating each of the five major musical genres in America. Each will be examined first in its cultural setting and then in its historical development.

A word of caution. The historical overlay dropped on to each sociocultural genre produces some thoughts which conflict with traditional labels. For example, Classic Jazz means to most people the early days of jazz, the 1920s, Louis Armstrong, *et al*. But in the system which follows, Louis Armstrong and the 1920s end up being called Baroque—because of the polyphonic activity, the polarity of voices, the inherent theatricality of the music, etc.

This kind of conflict with traditional labels happens only occasionally, though, and should not be too troublesome.

148

17

Classical
Music

The term "classical music" has appeared two ways throughout this book: (a) classical (with a small case "c") means that special kind of music performed by symphony orchestras, opera companies, ballet troupes, and so on, and (b) Classical (with a capital "C") means a special historical period within that broad category of music for symphony orchestras, opera companies, etc.

It is in the first sense that this chapter gets its title. The following several pages will be devoted exclusively to a discussion of that music which is clearly different from jazz, pop, gospel, rock, and such.

CULTURAL FRAME OF REFERENCE

Sociological Roots

By the 1600s, the history of classical music falls into the hands of North Central Europeans—in fact, by the Germans. After some earlier important contributions by a few non-Germans, the German influence begins to carry strong and steady: Heinrich Schutz (1585-1672), Johann Froberger

ILLUSTRATION: George Szell, Conductor. Courtesy of CBS Records.

(1616-1667), Johann Pachelbel (1653-1706), Dietrich Buxtehude (1637-1707), Johann Sebastian Bach (1685-1750), George Frideric Handel (1685-1759), Franz Joseph Haydn (1732-1809), Wolfgang Amadeus Mozart (1756-1791), Ludwig van Beethoven (1770-1827), Franz Schubert (1797-1828), Robert Schumann (1810-1856), Anton Bruckner (1824-1896), Johannes Brahms (1833-1897), Gustav Mahler (1860-1911), Richard Strauss (1864-1949), Max Reger (1873-1916), Arnold Schoenberg (1874-1951), Alban Berg (1885-1935), Paul Hindemith (1895-1963), Karlheinz Stockhausen (born 1928), and others. Certainly an impressive list of major contributors to the mainstream of classical music.

Not only were these Germans unusually productive and influential, but nearly all played a keyboard instrument—harpsichord, organ, or piano. This may account for the great value placed on architectural factors in the classical music of Western Culture.

Keyboard specialists tend to think more in linear and structural terms than in dramatic and coloristic terms. Linear thinking is also, of course, the result of the logical-sequential bias of what McLuhan calls the print culture society. The visual West has a very different kind of music from the tactile-aural East.

The music called "classical" has been produced, then, by and large, by a literate, articulate, constructivistic, Teutonic mentality. Among all the world's people—indeed, even among Western Civilization—this is a select community. The patrons and audiences have always been a select minority, too: first the Church, then individuals of royal and noble birth, and now the upper and upper-middle classes, with remarkable leadership provided by Jewish performers and conductors.

In America, things were totally dominated by the Eastern Seaboard crowd for a long time. In the past 30-40 years, though, strong and comprehensive classical music activities have grown up in Los Angeles, Chicago, Cleveland, and elsewhere.

Psychoemotional Traits

Classical music is supported, generally, by the business, professional, and intellectual citizens of America's larger cities. Among the most remarkable characteristics of this crowd of people is the concept of *time*—lapsic time.

Time is a valuable item in this culture. Time is a measurable commodity regulated and controlled by appointments, commitments, and schedules with tables and target dates—all in terms of weeks, months, and year-by-year implementation designs. Symphony orchestra conductors hire soloists three years in advance, as a normal routine, and the annotator prepares a full year's program notes during the summer, often. Such linear time-bound thinking is unheard of in Nashville, where time is a long range inexorable intangible, and, as a record executive was heard to say, "God only knows what'll be coming down six months from today." There are no printed programs for the Grand Ole Opry because even at 8:00 p.m. no one is really sure what the order of appearances will be for the 10:00 second show.

The world of classical music is generally conservative and stable. Sociologist Ian Robertson observes a willingness "to defer immediate gratification in the hope of greater future reward." Getting a college education, building a business on sound financial bases, mastering a foreign language—all these things require a capacity for deferred gratification.

Musical Results

It also requires a large capacity for deferred gratification to wait 44 measures before the second theme comes in in Movement I of Mozart's *Symphony No. 40.* And to wait until measure 59 for the second theme to come around in Movement I of Beethoven's *Symphony No. 5.* This kind of listening to music is an exercise in goal-directed aural discipline, and it requires some patience and control to develop.

The music is a constant search for increasing refinement and sophistication. The music mirrors the values which are held highest by the culture: elegance, propriety, reserve, control, continuous growth, goal-ordered development, and the like.

Topics of Concern

As might be expected, achievement topics abound in classical music, that is, topics having to do with overcoming obstacles or clarifying disorder of some kind. Love, Truth, Beauty, Justice, God, and Country always win over Evil, Ugliness, Hatred, and Injustice. Mythological, allegorical, and metaphorical symbols for strength, diligence, perseverence, and all the other Judaic-Christian values are everywhere present. The passions are larger than life.

HISTORICAL REVIEW

The special genre of music called classical music does not exist in all cultues: among the American Indians, the Eskimos, the natives of Ethiopia, and among many other past and current non-industrial cultures, for example, there is no distinction between folk music and classical music. Nor has classical music always existed in Western Culture. It is the product of modern civilization, and its growth and development parallels the growth and development of Western Civilization, reaching its peak in the third major period of the culture. Western Culture is often divided into three major epochs: (1) Antiquity—from earliest times to the end of the Roman Empire, (2) the Middle Ages—from 500 to 1450, and (3) Modern Society—from 1450 to the present. Nearly all the classical music heard by today's music appreciation students in recitals and concerts will come from the period of Modern Society, and most of it will have been written after the year 1700.

A word of caution in regard to the next several pages of discussion on historical periods. The terms (Classic, Romantic, *et al.*) come from art history which, like all the social sciences, drew its inspiration from the Darwinians who stressed the evolutionary developmental threads in an in-depth analysis of any given phenomenon. This is fine for explaining mountain ranges and the reason cocker spaniel puppies look like they do, but it is sometimes misleading in the arts—because it seems to suggest that Mozart was a less complex form of Beethoven who was a less complex form of Strauss, and so on.

There is a bit of truth in the above kind of thinking, but a much better approach is to think of music as a jewel with many polished surfaces, each flat surface reflecting the Truth and Beauty of the historical moment. As time progresses, a different face of the jewel comes into view, now Baroque, now the Classic, now the Romantic. Each reflection is full, in no way incomplete, and draws on the entire human condition as its base.

The Birth of the Genre. 500-1600.

It was not until the fall of the Roman Empire and the corresponding rise of the Catholic Church that trained musicians began to make a difference in the music of the land. Classical music took shape ever so slowly during two large historical periods: (a) The Middle Ages (500-1450) and (b) The Renaissance (1450-1600).

The Middle Ages (500-1450). Two subdivisions of the Middle Ages appear often in historical writing: (a) the Romanesque Period (500-1150) and (b) the Gothic Period (1150-1450).

In modern recitals and concerts there will be very few musical selections from the Romanesque Period, although a great many of the beautiful melodies in the liturgy of the Catholic Church have their origins here. Near the end of the Romanesque Period, several generations of musician-clerics at the abbey of St. Martial in Limoges, France, composed certain additions and parallel harmony parts to the great body of sacred melodic chant which Pope Gregory's scholars had collected and codified way back in the early days of the Romanesque Period. The additions were called *tropes*, and certain special tropes were called *sequences*. The parallel "harmony" parts were called *organum*, and the only thing close to that sound in today's music is the harmony part sometimes sung in country music, alternating in 4ths and 5ths.

Besides the work of the church musicians during the Romanesque Period, two different groups of secular musicians were at work in society. The first group, a class of minstrel entertainers, called *jongleurs* in France, *Gaukler* in Germany, and gleemen in England, roamed the countryside performing on a variety of musical instruments, throwing (juggling) small apples, catching knives, jumping through hoops, executing card tricks, and doing similar things to the delight of their audiences. These musician-entertainers, who later (14th century) settled down to form guilds and fraternities, were the direct ancestors of today's dance band musicians, symphony orchestra members, and touring rock groups.

A second group active near the end of the Romanesque Period, the *goliards*, dropped out of the universities of the day to wander around singing parodies and writing satiric poems about the Virgin Mary, about corruption in the Church, about hypocrisy in society, and about drinking, making love, and all other manner and variety of ribald behavior.In a very real sense, the *goliards* were the hippies of their day, singing about the same topics which upset the Haight-Asbury Crowd, living a life style similar to the Woodstock Generation, and playing the same general role in the society of the day.

The most famous collection of *goliard* tunes and poems, *Carmina Burana* (from the monastery, Benediktbeuren, in Germany, where the collection was found), contains thoughts which Bob Dylan and Joan Baez would have found acceptable and consistent with their careers. Even the original musical styles used to deliver these social criticisms are similar—short, irregular, modal melodies; simple and direct, spare, harmonies; skeletal accompaniment support on a lute or guitar; all delivered with razor-sharp understatement surface mannerisms.

The Gothic Period (1150-1450) of the Middle Ages brought new things in what eventually became the field of classical music. Church musicians continued to expand their work with the sacred chant of the Church, producing the *clausula*, the *polyphonic conductus*, and the *motet*. In the School of Notre Dame, two composers, Leonin and Perotin, stand out above the others. Religious music was well on its way to becoming one of the important arts used in the service of the Church.

In the secular world, three groups of musician-poets created a large body of love songs, spinning songs, laments, satires, epic tales of great deeds, and songs about knights wooing shepherd maidens. These poets—called *troubadours* in Southern France, called *trouveres* in Northern France, and called *Minnesingers* in Germany—were upper class citizens, and often hired jongleurs to actually perform their music. The tunes are delightful and sophisticated works. Nothing quite like these songs exists today. The only possibly similar works might be the hundreds of well-wrought show tunes of Kurt Weil, Cole Porter, and Stephen Sondheim.

Following the courtly poets by a hundred years or more was a different group, the *Meistersingers*, German burgher class citizens. With many pedantic rules, categories of membership, and a highly organized approach to all aspects of the musical enterprise, the *Meistersingers'* organizational scheme would correspond to, perhaps, something like the Masons today, and musically to something like the Society For the Preservation and Encouragement of Barbershop Quartet Singing in America.

Near the end of the Middle Ages, a sizable body of sacred and secular music was written by the Frenchman Guillaume de Machaut (1300-1377) and the Italian Francesco Landini (1325-1397). Machaut was a priest, but much involed in the affairs of the world. He spent most of his life as a musician and court official in the service of several wealthy families. In addition to many love songs and other secular works, Machaut wrote one of the first complete settings of the Mass. He wrote in the *ars nova*, the new artistic style, of the day, made possible by new notation practices.

Landini, a blind organist, wrote a few madrigals and caccias (hunting songs) and many ballatas (songs to accompany dances). For many years, Landini was organist at the Church of Lorenzo in Florence. He, too, wrote in the new style, and was well known as one of the best of the new and modern composers of the day.

The Renaissance (1450-1600). Historians often consider the Renaissance (Fr., meaning "rebirth") to be the beginning of modern history. Scholars assigned the term to the age because of what they saw as a rebirth of learning after a period of intellectual darkness. Newer interpretations recognize a sudden increase in academic and artistic matters, but acknowledge all the previous intellectual activities which had obtained, especially in the Church, during the Middle Ages.

A convenient date for the beginning of the Renaissance is 1450—during which year Johann Gutenberg and Johann Fust formed a partnership to start a printing house. Three years later Constantinople fell to the Ottoman Turks sending thousands of Byzantine scholars fleeing Westward. Soon an intellectual-scientific-artistic movement began which eventually led to the Protestant Reformation, the Age of Enlightenment, and the Industrial Revolution. And to the field of classical music as it is known today.

The well-known activities of Ferdinand Magellan (1480-1521), Leonardo da Vinci (1452-1519), Michelangelo Buonarroti (1475-1564), Desiderius Erasmus (1466-1536), Francois Rabelais (1494-1553), and many others gave the Renaissance a strong and colorful early period. Josquin des Prez (1450-1521) brought music to new heights, with his great skills and imagination. He wrote masses, motets, and secular vocal pieces, and was Martin Luther's favorite composer. He was especially adept at writing imitative counterpoint.

Heard more often today are the works of Giovanni Pierluigi da Palestrina (1525-1594) who wrote almost exclusively for religious purposes, masses, motets, and other religious works. Palestrina responded to the decisions made at the Council of Trent (1545-1563), and wrote music of great spiritual depth and beauty while avoiding the earthy sounds which had been creeping into religious music. His great output is studied even today as the model for the best 16th century counterpoint.

Perhaps the most versatile composer of the Renaissance was Orlando di Lasso (1532-1594). Lasso wrote some 2,000 compositions in all manner of secular and sacred forms, masses, motets, Italian madrigals, German lieder, French chansons, and magnificats. He showed great singing talent at a very early age, and his voice was so beautiful that he was kidnapped three times to be placed in different choirs. After many early successes throughout Europe, he settled in Munich to become Emperor Maximilian's favorite composer.

Renaissance music was surely not all vocal, but many of the extended works in manuscript which have survived are vocal pieces. This music tends to be gentle-flowing without bombastic rhythmic pulsations and without firm meter beats. It is linear music, with each voice doing its job independently. Dissonances are usually prepared so there are no "harsh" moments of any duration in the music, but, rather, beautiful waves of tension and relaxation.

Instruments were crude by today's standard, but instrumental music seems to have been extremely colorful and varied. Small groups of mixed instruments were probably the norm, even though full families of viols and recorders were available. The art of classical music as it is known and loved today was clearly taking shape and emerging as a distinct professional discipline.

Not much is known about the music of the common folk. Surely there were vigorous dances and lusty ballads delivered by the lads and lasses in the taverns of the day. And weddings, funerals, picnics, and impromptu celebrations among the street people and rural peasants certainly called for music, then, as now.

The Baroque Era. 1600-1750.

The term *baroque* is borrowed from art history (as was the term *renaissance*) to indicate that the music was demonstrably different from that which preceded it. The word *barroco* means "misshaped pearl," and scholars at first considered the Baroque Period in the arts to have been an unfortunate degeneration of the beautiful days of the Renaissance. Even today, the term Baroque has a certain connotation of "big and gaudy."

Dozens of important composers worked in the Baroque, but by all odds, George Frideric Handel (1685-1759) and Johann Sebastian Bach (1685-1750) are the most important and the most often heard in concert halls today. Bach was not considered that important by his contemporaries. Indeed, it was not until Mendelssohn rediscovered Bach in the early 1800s that Bach's rightful place was established in the history of classical music.

Handel was a successful and well known man of the world whose compositions were much appreciated by the society of the day. At the age of 27, he settled in England and began to cultivate his already illustrious reputation as an opera composer. Handel's fortunes rose and fell with the popularity of opera in England, until he finally abandoned opera completely, and turned his attention to oratorios and chamber music.

Baroque music has a sweep and grandeur to it that clearly marks it as coming from the age of world exploration, the rise of the middle classes, the emergence of the modern European nations, the invention of the steam engine, the discovery of the law of gravity, and other such things. The music is full of contrasts: contrasts in tempo, contrasts in dynamics, contrasts in musical forces at work. It is theatrical music, with plenty of built-in drama.

The difference between vocal and instrumental music began to disappear, in strict musical terms, and there was no significant difference between the kind of harmony, melody, and rhythm used by Handel for the voices in the *Messiah*, as opposed to the harmony, melody, and rhythm used for the orchestral instruments. Baroque vocal music is, therefore, difficult to sing, quite often.

Instrumental groups got a little larger. The violin family replaced the viol family. The transverse flute replaced the recorder. The harpsichord replaced the clavichord. Mixed instrumental groups were the rule, although there was a tendency to make the string section the main body of the orchestral sound.

The Classic Period. 1750-1820.

The massive huffing and puffing of the Baroque soon gave way to an urge toward refinement and restraint. This was the age of elegance, simplicity, control, objectivity—The Age of Reason: Voltaire, Beaumarchais, Kant, and the first edition of the *Encyclopedia Britannica*. The sophistication and charm was a veneer over the smoldering fires of enormous social unrest, of course, but all the same it was a short and beautiful age of classical purity.

Franz Joseph Haydn (1732-1809) and Wolfgang Amadeus Mozart (1756-1791) stand out as the purest of the purists in the Classic Period. Their music will be always dignified and reserved. The passion will be there, but in a properly controlled delivery. The melodies are lyric and songlike. The harmonies are clean and clear, and the cadences are a bit more frequent than in Baroque music. The musical forms are neat, symmetrical, and easily grasped.

Homophonic texture began to replace polyphonic texture as the way to do things. The piano replaced the harpsichord. The brasses and woodwinds were still primitive, but more and more in evidence, now. String quartets appeared. Chamber groups. Opera, as it is now known and loved. Most important, the orchestra emerged pretty much as it is now, only smaller, of course: a full string section of violins (first and second), violas, cellos, and double basses, with some woodwinds and brasses, plus an occasional timpani.

The Romantic Period. 1820-1900.

That giant among giants, Ludwig van Beethoven (1770-1827) stood boldly with one foot in the Classic Period and one foot in the Romantic Period. His music has all the designs of Classicism (control, balance, order, etc.), but at every turn he pops the buttons off the Classical garment with his ferocious emotional energies. All the flamboyant things the later Romantics would do can be felt bubbling below the surface of Beethoven's music.

It was a different age, an age of explosive growth for Industrial Man. Steamships, the American Civil War, Henrik Ibsen, Charles Dickens, World's Fairs, factories, inventions all over the place, and the rise of nationalistic thinking among the European peoples. This was a new age, indeed.

Beethoven, Franz Liszt (1811-1886), Hector Berlioz (1803-1869), and Richard Wagner (1831-1883) banished forever any thoughts that composers ought to be decent responsible human beings. They said, wrote, and did things that Mozart and Haydn would never have considered possible. The whole notion of the artist as a "creator" above and beyond the normal laws of society got firmly lodged in the Occidental Brain at this time. Composers, virtuoso soloists, and conductors developed the super-star mentality so common even today in the world of the concert hall. All of which was, of course, perfectly in keeping with the tenor of the age.

The music is also bigger than life, with massive orchestras, bombastic climaxes, endlessly shifting harmonies, and bold exotic colors everywhere present. Gone are the delicate phrases of Mozart. Gone are the intellectual delights of refinement and control. Things are big and bold and passionate, now. The iron frame of the grand piano gave it tons of tension and mountains of rich sonorities to challenge the new tubas, bass trombones, percussion instruments, and all.

Grandiose operations are the rule: operas inflate to mind-boggling dimensions in music and pageantry; orchestras grow to monster proportions; personalities and careers bedazzle the entire world of music. Right along side this movement, a kind of parallel movement occurs in which things get very intimate: piano recitals in small salons for only a few invited guests, for example. Things are either very big or very small. The unashamed emotionalism is present, though, in either case.

The Romantic Age came to a final fling at the end of the century with each country seemingly bent on declaring itself in its own unique terms. This is undoubtedly a manifestation of the same forces which eventually brought on World War I, and is probably a lot deeper than the traditional socioeconomic causes so superficially offered. Whatever these profound stirrings in Occidental Culture were, they produced a whole crowd of Russians (Glinka, Borodin, Cui, Mussorgsky, Balakirev, Rimsky-Korsakov, Tchaikovsky), Czechs (Smetana and Dvorak), Hungarians (Liszt, Bartok, Kodaly), Spaniards (Albeniz, Granados, de Falla), Scandinavians (Grieg, Siebelius), and Frenchmen (Debussy and Ravel) who cultivated assiduously the particular musical traits they felt to be special to their national origins.

The Russians, Czechs, and others are called Nationalist composers. The French version of this movement, often given a style category of its own, was *Impressionism*. The Impressionist composers gave the world a beautiful musical realization of the abstruse multiplicity of the French mentality, language, and life style. Claude Debussy (1862-1918) and Maurice Ravel (1875-1937) led the way, with Debussy being the more daring, innovative and blissfully poetic of the two.

Musically, the Impressionists carried the Romantic aesthetic to its logical conclusion—no calculated form, no predictable gestures, just pure emotions and sensations cast up for their own pleasures. Shimmering pools of sounds, diaphonous cascades of delicate notes, endless non-developmental patterns of colors and "impressions."

The Early 20th Century. 1900-1950.

The cataclysmic redefinition of itself which Western Civilization called World War I was revealed in the arts, of course, long before and long after the actual killing-pruning of the species and the imperative bargaining over territories. McLuhan says, "War is Education." By this he means that war is a highly condensed, indeed explosive, form of changing the behavior of a culture—of bringing the behavior in line with the real psychic needs and desires of the tribe, without waiting for the older mores and institutions to die natural deaths.

McLuhan also says that the artists are the antennae of the species: the artists see and feel the real inner life of a society with much greater depth and clarity than the masses, and the artists cast up their observations in their special language—painting, poetry, sculpture, music, photography, the novel, and so on. The events of the early 20th Century certainly make sense when interpreted in the light of McLuhan's provocative thesis.

Western Culture went through a blinding storm of "isms" in the arts. The artists were searching for the appropriate expression of what they felt to be the core of reality: futurism, folklorism, barbarism, cubism, expression-ism, brutism, dadaism, neo-classicism, neo-romanticism, intellectualism, serialism, pluralism, and everything in the book. The world, at least the Judaic-Christian World, had trouble with itself, and the music of the first half of the century clearly reflects all these divergent pulls and stresses.

By far, the most famous of the new composers was Igor Stravinsky (1882-1971), catapulted into the international spotlight by the controversial works for ballet he wrote in the very early days of the century. His *Rite of Spring* caused a riot in Paris when it was first performed in 1913. The composer, then 31 years old, was launched on one of the biggest careers in the business.

Arnold Schoenberg (1874-1951), equally controversial but much less influential with important patrons of the arts, spent his life in partial frustration and disappointment over the failure of society-at-large to accept, or even fully understand, his method of composition. The "method" was just that, a unique system of using all 12 tones as equal, autonomous components in the creation of the raw materials of music: scales, melodies, harmonies, and all. There was no familiar comfortable return to a recognizable home base. The music obeyed a rigorous discipline, yes, but the system was so complex and involved that the listener, even the experienced and knowledgeable listener, had a difficult time with it. The system, known as twelve-tone music, or dodecaphonic music, or serial music, is still around today, but suffers a bit from the enormous interest in electronic things.

The orchestra got terribly large or terribly small in the early 1900s. Harmony, melody, rhythm, tone, texture, and expressive devices got pushed to the limits of human endurance. Experimentation was everywhere, especially in the area of form: the question was, how to create a cohesive, coherent musical experience without using the traditional A-B, A-B-A, sonata-allegro, and other designs. There was an intense search for some kind of organic logic outside the traditional procedures of musical composition.

Composers swam out into strange waters. Some remained conservative in basic approach: Ralph Vaughan Williams (1872-1958), Paul Hindemith (1895-1963), Aaron Copland (b. 1900), and many others. Other composers followed Schoenberg's controversial 12-tone techniques: Anton Webern (1883-1945) and Alban Berg (1885-1935). Some modernists, Stravinsky, for one, went through a neo-classical period. Samuel Barber (b. 1910), Norman Dello Joio (b. 1913), and Howard Hanson (1896-1981) have been called neoromantics. The times were colorful indeed.

Modern Music. 1950 to the Present.

Just as World War I was felt most keenly, and expressed most passionately, by the artists of the day, so too was World War II. In addition, the new advances in communications made all developments immediately available to the entire world in a matter of hours. The H Bomb Mentality, the Race for Space, Suburbia U.S.A., the Baby Boom, dozens of crises in social and economic areas, and wild shifts in political power are all reflected in the music of the times.

Two major trends are evident: a move toward greater control over the musical sounds by the composer of those sounds; and an effort to introduce great freedom, that is to say, indeterminancy, into the musical experience.

Control. Some composers have extended Schoenberg's technique to include not only tones, but all other components —time, tone, color, dynamics, the works. Ernst Krenek's (b. 1900) *Sestina* sets out to control everything. Pierre Boulez (b. 1925) does the same in several works.

Total control of what happens musically can be brought about through mathematical principles (Iannis Zenakis [b. 1922]), or computers (J.K. Randall [b. 1929]), or synthesizers (Milton Babbit [b. 1916]), or tape recorders (Edgard Varese [1883-1965]), and combinations of these and other techniques. An interesting kind of total control over sounds which were once free is *musique concrete*. Natural sounds—bird calls, steam engines, flutes, violins, jack hammers, rustling leaves, human sounds—are recorded on tape, then altered in whatever imaginary way the composer so desires, by playing the tape in reverse, say, or at half speed, or filtering out certain partials, or such.

Freedom. Some composers want to be surprised, and want their listeners to be surprised, each time, by the musical experience. Chance music (aleatoric) it is called. John Cage (b. 1912) is among the best known workers in this field. His *Imaginary Landscape No. 4* (1951) for 12 radios still causes quite a stir when it is performed.

Lucas Foss (b. 1922) has cultivated the technique of improvisation in several works so that the performers have several options at any given moment on what sound patterns to deliver. All manner of "chance" techniques have been used, including rolling dice, squirting ink on a blank music paper, having ants crawl over an ink pad then onto a sheet of music paper, shuffling cards on which brief note patterns are printed, and other such curious innovations.

In most of this new music, there are no such things as melody, harmony, form, counterpoint, and rhythms in the traditional sense, but, rather, a continuously changing array of acoustical sensations which the composer offers to the audience. Tempers run high, here, too, since the listeners sometimes feel they are being made fools of, and the composers feel they have been grossly misunderstood.

A curious return to traditional melodies and harmonies appeared in the 1960s and 1970s and has become fashionable in the 1980s. Called *minimalism*, the music consists of short melodic fragments, simple chords, and conservative rhythmic groupings—all delivered in hypnotic repetition. The effect is rather like a needle stuck in the groove of a long-play recoding.

Among the more popular exponents of the new style and technique are Steve Reich (b. 1938), composer of *Music for 18 Musicians* (1976), *Octet* (1979), and *Tehillim*; Philip Glass (b. 1938) best known for his *Einstein on the Beach*; and Terry Riley (b. 1936), the elder statesman of the field, whose *In C* (1964) consists of 53 melodic fragments played at will in any order by any number of instruments in any combination available.

Rock musicians have picked up some of the minimalists' style and spirit, Mike Oldfield on his *Tubular Bells* (1973) and Brian Eno in his recent works, most notably the *Airport Music*.

All in all, the new musical activities in the world of classical music are as exciting now as they were when Hector Berlioz was so severely criticized for his innovations. While the current battles rage among music critics, composers, performers, theorists, informed classical music lovers, and conductors, the real action is going on in the background music to the *Star Wars* movie series, in the sound tracks of the savage horror films, in the bleeps of all the computers so abundant, and in the sounds generated in the Space Game Arcades all over the land. These radical new sound environments are here to stay. They become the subliminal preparation for what listeners will or will not accept in the future, so most of the judgments by scholars and critics are academic.

18

Afro-American Music

The varieties of black music in America defy classification. At different times, the terms Blues, Gospel, Rhythm and Blues, Rock 'n' Roll, Be-Bop, Cool School, West Coast Jazz, Progressive Jazz, Ragtime, Boogie Woogie, Dixieland, Gut-Bucket, Kansas City, Soul, Motown, Urban Blues, and many others have been used to refer to that special Afro-American socioanthropological musical subculture so clearly summarized by the generic term *Jazz*.

It is fashionable, these days, to show an interest in jazz. In contrast to country music, jazz enjoys a certain acceptance and even occasional prestige in music circles. Jazz courses are springing up in the colleges of the nation, jazz musicians now score background music for TV and the movies, and university deans are appointing jazz composers and musicians to their music departments. It has been a long time coming, but it is finally here.

ILLUSTRATION: Edward "Duke" Ellington. Courtesy of CBS Records.

It was not this way, just a few decades ago. In 1925, the editor of *Etude* magazine warned that "in its sinister aspects, jazz is doing a vast amount of harm to young minds and bodies not yet developed to resist temptation." Around the same time, Coach Knox, of Harvard, reported that the boys were coming to him with "hollow chests" and "spindle legs," and he was sure that jazz was the cause of it all. In 1934, Monseigneur Conefrey saw a sinister plot in jazz: "Jazz was borrowed from Central Africa by a gang of wealthy international Bolshevists from America, and their aim is to strike at the Christian civilization through the world."[1]

CULTURAL FRAME OF REFERENCE

Sociological Roots

Jazz comes from a mixture of West African and European life styles as this mixture grew up in the plantations of the South, at first, and later in the inner-city ghettos of the North and East. The music which evolved out of this strange cultural mix has puzzled scholars for years.

West African and European musical systems are not as different as people generally believe. There is some three- and four-part singing among the Ashanti tribe, for example, rather like Anglo-Saxon hymn singing. West Africans practice a "call and response" delivery, not unlike the colonists' "deaconing" or "lining out" of a hymn (the preacher or deacon sang a line of the hymn, the congregation answered with the same line, and they went through the entire hymn in this manner). Both West African and European religious ceremonies get rather emotional, at times, also, and music plays a big role in these highly charged affairs.

Whatever may be the differences and similarities between the two cultures which gave birth to jazz, there can be no doubt that the black element of the synthesis has been, and is, the dominant factor. Jazz is essentially a black interpretation of the American experiment, an absolutely unique thing which could probably not have happened between the European colonists and any other culture. Suppose, for example, by some historical turn of events, the colonists had enslaved a large number of Orientals to work the cotton plantations. It is highly unlikely that authentic Japanese, or Chinese, music would have fused with European music to result in an Oriental version of "St. Louis Blues." It is nearly inconceivable. The musical systems, and the life styles, are simply too far apart.

Psychoemotional Traits

In 1966, sociologist Charles Keil put an end to a lot of nonsense about black psychoemotional and self-identity issues. Keil explains that to explore Afro-American music without exploring the culture of poverty is pointless. He then explains that what most sociologists have learned, first-hand, about black culture must be considered most cautiously because, "Almost any Negro in the presence of a white or black bourgeois interviewer or social worker can recite a stream of conventional American values and beliefs without a hitch, halt, or second thought."[2]

He continues, "Yet it is also true that these are rarely the cultural guidelines by which the person reciting them lives. The art of the 'put on' has of necessity been developed to an exceptionally high level in Negro culture...." After clarifying that the study is essentially a study not of race, or genetics, or biology, or color, or any other thing so often sought, but rather a study of "slum culture" or "underculture," and after setting the alert for the "put-on," Keil documents rather clearly the following general observations about this "urban culture of poverty."[3]

First, the culture is predominantly auditory and tactile rather than visual and literate. Second, kinship patterns may be Western, but one of the most striking features of black social structure is the battle of the sexes. Third, traditional Protestantism—thrift, sobriety, "inner-directedness," strictly codified sexual behavior, and a strong insistence on respectability—tend "to be reversed in the Negro cultural framework." Fourth, "time and historical sense" are vague and undefined: "The black man on the street corner, like most slum dwellers everywhere, lives for the present and tends to drift with events rather than show up for appointments assuming that he has any."[4]

Musical Results

Jazz is highly emotional and complex music, to be sure. There is a certain translucence about the whole art, as compared with, say, country music. Harmonies are rich and complicated and extended; melodies are constantly embellished and changed and re-worked; rhythms are in a continuous state of mutation and rebirth; the sheer sound of the voices and instruments is not fixed at all, but constantly evolving.

Forms are closed and non-architectural. No long-range 40-minute concertos, here, but, rather, constant exploration of shifting centers of emotional reality. No extended patterns of sequential and developmental musical gestures, but, rather, continuous re-working of kaleidoscopic clusters of melodic and harmonic materials. Harmony, especially, is different, in jazz. It is a dramatic thing in jazz, rather than the structural thing it is in classical European music.

And improvisation is at the heart of it all. Continuous, spontaneous, and intense. Always searching for the most expressive way to communicate within the prescribed musical conventions.

Topics of Concern

Religion is big. Always has been. Charles Keil cautions against considering this as the typical Protestant middle class religious practice, however, "Speaking in tongues, prophecy, healing, trance, 'possession,' a staff of nurses to assist those 'filled with the Holy Ghost,' frenzied dancing, hand clapping, tambourine playing, instrumental groups, fluctuating musical styles, singing-screaming sermons, constant audience participation—these and other features of Negro church services are completely foreign to the prevailing conception of Protestantism."[5]

Love is a big topic, of course, not only in jazz, but in all musical fields. The kind of love expressed in jazz is slightly different, though, from the late Marty Robbins singing "My Woman, My Woman, My Wife." In black music, there is a realistic bitter-sweet realization of the frailty and impermanence of love, a guarded ambivalence about the whole thing.

The blues, as a life style—the state of being excluded from the mainstream of American society—provides a philosophical base for an enormous body of jazz. It has been going on since the plantation days, and will continue until the socioeconomic picture changes. As LeRoi Jones has said, "Negro music is essentially the expression of an attitude, or a collection of attitudes, about the world, and only secondarily an attitude about the way the music is made."[6]

The sportin' life also gets a big play in black music. contrary to white middle class sociologists' thoughts about cultural norms, this concern with cars and suits and women is not some kind of abnormal behavior, but, as Keil says, "If we are ever to understand what urban Negro culture is all about, we had best view entertainers and hustlers as culture heroes—integral parts of the whole [culture]—rather than as deviants or shadow figures."[7]

HISTORICAL REVIEW

The first slaves landed on American shores in 1619, and for nearly 300 years thereafter, very little is known about authentic black musical practices. Fragmentary evidence found in colonial diaries and journals suggests that plantation life was rich in musical occasions, and that the blacks also fiddled and sang for their white masters.[8] It was not until after the Emancipation Proclamation, however, that the field of jazz, as it is now known, began to take shape. The minstrel show (the white man's effort to characterize, and capitalize on, black music) was dying out, and the real article, genuine black music, was beginning to appear as a visible commodity in the mainstream of American society.

The Birth of the Genre. Blues and Ragtime. 1890-1917.

If the Renaissance in classical music was a kind of "emergence of the art as it is known today," so too were the early days of jazz. Composers and performers began to practice their trade to the exclusion of other subsistence skills. The music lost its strictly utilitarian function and became a product to be marketed for gain. The purity of the art in both classical music and jazz is striking. At the risk of wild generalization, it might be said that what Palestrina is to classical music, the blues is to jazz.

Contrary to popular belief, New Orleans was not the only location of early jazz activities. Jazz was everywhere: New York, Boston, Philadelphia, and even out on the West Coast. New Orleans was, of course, the first home of King Oliver, Louis Armstrong, Bunk Johnson, and many others, but Willy "The Lion" Smith, Duke Ellington, Fats Waller, and Fletcher Henderson had no sustained contact at all with things in New Orleans. Two large areas of jazz flowered: the blues, essentially vocal, and ragtime, essentially instrumental.

The Blues

Elizabethan folks had the "blue devils" when they felt unexplainably melancholy. The term seems to have lingered in the American colonies, and appeared in the late 1800s among the black community as "the blues." Before long the term meant very much what it does today—a musical expression of that melancholy feeling which comes from loneliness, loss of a loved one, lack of money, and other forms of sadness.

Blues scholars speak of major distinctions between and among early blues.[9] The following four areas or four large categories might be sketched out: (a) Country Blues—with several subdivisions to cover the activities of Charley Patton (Mississippi 1887-1929), Blind Lemon Jefferson (Texas 1897-1929), and many others all the way from South Carolina to Texas and up through Tennessee, (b) Classic Blues—to refer to Gertrude "Ma" Rainey (1886-1939), Bessie Smith (1894-1937), Bertha "Chippie" Hill (1905-1950), and all those men and women who flourished in the 1920s, (c) Urban Blues—Lonnie Johnson (1889-1970), Roosevelt Sykes (b. 1906), B. B. King (b. 1925), *et al.*, and (d) Rhythm and Blues—a synthesis of all that had preceded, now (1940 and thereafter) mixed with amplified instruments, drums, dancing, big-time record sales, and the like.

Delivered in a rhymed couplet, with the first line repeated, the blues—poignant, bitter-sweet, powerfully moving lamentations on life's endless woes—function as a kind

170

of secular version of the well documented black spiritual. Even the most modern of the highly educated contemporary jazz musicians quench their thirst in the eternal waters of the blues when they run dry.

Ragtime

A cross between European military march forms and sportin' house piano styles swept through America in the late 1800s and early 1900s. The new craze, called Ragtime (from, perhaps, "ragged" time), attracted Tin Pan Alley composers Irving Berlin and George Gershwin as well as classical composers Igor Stravinsky and Darius Milhaud, and Paul Hindemith.

The real article, though, the genuine thing, came from the Missouri-based pianist-composer Scott Joplin (1968-1917), pianist and bar owner Tom Turpin (1873-1922), and other bordello pianists. Joplin stood head and shoulders above the crowd, writing a detailed and successful teaching manual so classically trained pianists could learn to play and teach the new music, composing two ragtime operas (one lost, and the other, *Treemonisha*, done several times in the past few years), and carrying the torch high through his entire illustrious career. He considered ragtime to be America's real classical music, corresponding to the piano works of, say, Frederic Chopin, the European pianist-composer.[10]

Ragtime pianists came back into fashion in 1974 when Joplin's "Entertainer" was used in the Hollywood film *The Sting*. The last of the great ragtime pianists, Eubie Blake, died at the age of 100, in 1983.

The Baroque Era in Jazz. Dixieland. 1917-1930.

On January 26, 1917, the Original Dixieland Jazz Band opened an engagement at Reisenweber's Cabaret in New York. Scott Joplin died the same year, and the red-light district, Storyville, was closed in New Orleans. A new age had begun.

The music of this new era, called Dixieland, was and is strikingly similar to Baroque music in the classical field— polarity of outer voices, consistent motor drive, continuous polyphonic activity, terrace dymanics, and sectional closed forms. Even the socioeconomic circumstances: the speakeasies, the Chicago gangsters, bathtub gin, the flapper, and the raccoon coat. Surely the Roarin' 20s were Baroque in spirit and style.

Several geographic centers drew the best musicians for long periods of residence. Chicago, Kansas City, and New York began to compete with New Orleans for jazz activities. For a while in the 1920s, Chicago was decidedly the most exciting and productive spot in America. Joe "King" Oliver (1885-1938) and Louis Armstrong (1900-1971) drove their listeners wild exchanging cornet licks in the new style. Then, as now, personnel changes occurred often. Armstrong left Oliver in 1924, along with pianist Lil Hardin, clarinettist Johnny Dodds, and his brother, drummer Warren "Baby" Dodds. Oliver came back a year later with an impressive group which he called the Dixie Syncopators.

Equally impressive were the musicians who worked with Ferdinand Joseph La Menthe "Jelly Roll" Morton (1885-1941). The Red Hot Peppers made some of the best Dixieland recordings to come out of the 1920s. Jelly Roll's piano work on these sides is a marvel of invention and rhythmic drive.

A typical Dixieland group would have six musicians, or so: piano, drums, bass, cornet, clarinet, and trombone was a common ensemble. The music was highly contrapuntal to the delight of musicians and audiences alike. The cornet carried the melody loud and clear, the clarinet decorated things with embellishments and filigree, and the trombone played countermelodies in the basement.

The Classic Period in Jazz. Big Bands. 1930-1945.

In the 1930s and 1940s, jazz went through an extraordinary rise in popularity, commercial success, and artistic growth. Big bands—the "classical orchestras" of the field of jazz— were playing the new "swing" music everywhere. This new music was and is classical in every sense: balanced, symmetric, nicely disciplined, a judicious mix of passion and reason, elegant and refined, controlled, and cerebral in a gentle way. Classical.

172

The big bands were a logical extension of the things Duke Ellington and Fletcher Henderson had been doing in the 1920s, of course. Ellington and Henderson had always thought in terms of sections of instruments and orchestral sounds, even early in their careers. On a deeper level, though, the big bands were a musical answer to some very profound changes in American society.

The repeal of prohibition in 1933 made the speakeasies obsolete, overnight. Night club entertainment could move out into the open, and it did. It moved into gigantic ballroom pavilions where a mere five or six piece Dixieland group was too small to do the job. The big bands moved into this picture, and ballroom dancing had spasms of "jitter-bugging" and other things to give its critics and supporters plenty to discuss.

Radio was really going big, also, in the 1930s, with *Your Lucky Strike Hit Parade* among the leading weekly programs. McLuhan says that radio tends to tribalize a culture, to destroy regional differences within a large territory, to lead a society into a collective mentality. America was certainly ready to be led into something to believe in, collectively—some kind of national frame of reference. America needed some idols, some models, some ideals. It is not just a coincidence that Kate Smith, Joe Dimaggio, Benny Goodman, General Motors, Bing Crosby, and the Hollywood Dream all emerged big in the 1930s.

The big band is a precision-tooled assembly-line General Motors approach to jazz. The brass section, reed section, and rhythm section work efficiently and effectively, each with specifically prescribed functions, each with a musical assignment to be executed. What a difference this was from the free blowing, elbow-flapping days of the Dixieland groups.

The big band could wallop a tune across a stadium-sized ballroom, and that was important. With 4 saxophones, 3-4 trombones, 3-4 trumpets, piano, bass, drums, guitar, boy singer, girl singer, vocal group, and a small band within the big band, the whole ensemble could make a lot of noise. The rhythm section (piano, bass, guitar, and drums) was situated together so the foundation of the band was firmly anchored in one spot. The weaker sounds of the saxophones had to be out front; the trombones had to be protected in the second row—so the dancers could not come up and pull the slide off the player's instrument; and the piercing and penetrating trumpets were across the back row. The leader-virtuoso was out front, like a musical version of a football quarterback.

The band within a band was common, too. Little groups came out of the big band proper. Benny Goodman has his trio, quartet, or sextet, as the spirit moved him. Artie Shaw had the Gramercy Five. Tommy Dorsey had the Clambake Seven. Bob Crosby had the Bobcats. These little groups consisted of the more theatrical virtuosos from the sections of the big band itself. Then there were the handsome boy singers, the pretty girl singers, the novelty numbers, and the short comedy routines. Put them all together, and they spell Trianon Ballroom, Chicago, 1939—a whole evening of entertainment.

The Romantic Period in Jazz. The Be-Bop Revolution. 1945-1960.

The glorious days of the classical big bands were numbered, though, and as the Second World War came to an end, the big bands went out of fashion. Gone were the neatly balanced phrases and controlled nuances of swing. The new stuff was explosive, passionate, and openly emotional. Romantic.

The black American had been off to fight a war for freedom, and returned home only to ride in the back of the bus. The blacks (especially Duke Ellington and Fletcher Henderson [often called the Father of Big Bands]), had given form to big band jazz, and white band leaders got wealthy and famous, while the black innovator had to enter the big hotel ballroom through the back door. The blacks just didn't have the financial connections to profit from their art, so they were at the mercy of the white business community for bookings, recording dates, copyright protection, publicity releases, and all the other complex aspects of the big band entertainment field.

There appeared in New York a group of angry young black musical militants who turned inward to themselves and their art. They were hostile, and disillusioned, and ferociously intellectual about their music. And they were determined not to be exploited by the white business community this time.

174

There is more to the story than just some hot-blooded revolutionaries in New York, though. America was a different place, now. Very different from the pre-war era. Suburbia was putting an end to the downtown metropolitan night life. As the suburbs grew, the local cocktail lounges and neighborhood show bars assumed greater significance in the industry. The invention of the automatic pin setter allowed bowling alleys to stay open all night long, and this cut into the all-night dancing crowd. The wartime surcharge on all night-club entertainment cut deeply into the musician's potential market. Large-scale financial woes beset the leaders of the big bands. The big bands came tumbling down. In December, 1946, these bands went under: Benny Goodman, Woody Herman, Harry James, Tommy Dorsey, Les Brown, Jack Teagarden, Benny Carter, and Ina Ray Hutton. Several came back, but on different terms. America was simply a very different society in the late 1940s.

The new thing—sociologically, musically, aesthetically, financially—was a small, intimate, intellectual combo. The period came to be known as the Be-Bop Revolution, taking its name, scholars thing, from the scat syllables used by some of the singers of the day. This bop style is similar in certain ways, to the days of the individualistic Dixieland band. Five or six instruments. Much soloistic improvisation. Small club atmosphere. A chamber music approach to things all the way.

Two distinct subschools grew out of the bop revolution: (a) the East coast, hot-blooded, intellectual, angular, difficult, complex, esoteric, introverted school, and (b) the West Coast, much more subdued, equally intellectual, less hostile, the "cool" school, as it was called. In addition to the two major styles there was a "progressive" style much in evidence. Thelonius Monk, Charlie Parker, and Dizzy Gillespie led the East Coast crowd. Gerry Mulligan, Chet Baker, Shorty Rogers and some others carried the West Coast style most successfully. Dave Brubeck was most frequently cited as a leader in the progressive manner of playing jazz. The progressive style was considered by the purists to be a little too clinical and academic.

At this same time there was much talk about a Third Stream kind of music. A mixing of the two large streams of music in America—classical and jazz—into a third stream which would have the best characteristics of each of the other two. Gunther Schuller, composer, scholar, horn player, conductor, a kind of Renaissance man of music, spoke often of Third Stream music and wrote several compositions which draw on both jazz and classical traditions.

ILLUSTRATION: Charles "Bird" Parker. Courtesy of Electra Records.

The Modern Period in Jazz. Funk, Free Form, and Fusion. 1960-Present.

Just as 20th century classical music seems to fall into two distinct periods (Early 20th Century [1900-1950] and Modern Music [1950-present]), so does it seem to happen in jazz.

(A) The *first period*, 1960-1969 corresponds remarkably with the days of Stravinsky and Schoenberg, a time of much experimentation and searching. In jazz, two things happened.

First. Jazz took a turn back toward its roots. These were the days of Marlon Brando, the urban folk song movement, Ray Charles, and other elemental forces at work in society. Jazz musicians and audiences began to tire of the cerebral intensity of the be-boppers, and an urge toward simplification was felt by members of the new Funky school. Led by pianist Horace Silver, alto saxophonist Julian "Cannonball" Adderly, and drummer Art Blakey, the return to blues, gospel, and less cerebral-more earthy sounds brought new vigor and excitement to the world of jazz. This same celebration of the essential blackness of the musical art came to be called Soul shortly after.

Second. Almost the reverse happened too. Free Form Jazz, as some called it, took off in the opposite direction—not back home to the blues and gospel feeling, but farther out into intellectual space. No prescribed melody. No pre-arranged chord patterns. No formal design. Total spontaneous improvisation at all times, or nearly so. This was the jazz musicians' answer to the Theater of the Absurd, to the nonbook writers, to Jackson Pollack and painter friends. The results were similarly striking and controversial. Ornette Coleman and Cecil Taylor suffered much criticism for their bold rejection of the traditional principles of jazz. Even the be-boppers (revolutionaries in their day) cried out in anguish at the Free Form sounds.

(B) The *second period*, 1969-present, opens with Miles Davis' historic recording, *Bitches Brew*. All this electronic stuff was a radical departure from Davis' mainstream be-bop career, and it launched a new ship into the deep waters of jazz. Indeed, more than anyone else, Miles can be called the Father of Fusion—that rich mixture of jazz and rock which has so dominated the jazz-rock scene since the early 1970s.

Fusion delivers no clean and neat 32-bar turnes, but rather explores the disco mentality of continuous ostinato patterns supporting extended free improvisatory offerings. Mix these techniques with the diverse sounds of the new electronic instruments, replace the old tunes with loosely conceived poetic concepts, put it all on a stage rather than in a dance hall, and a new art form takes shape.

To the fusion of traditional jazz and rock have been added certain Latin nuances, producing *salsa*. Every ten years or so, there seems to be a mixture of Afro-American jazz and Latin Amercan musical flavors: Dizzy Gillespie and Chano Pozo in the 1940s; Bud Shank and Laurindo Almeida in the 1950s; Stan Getz and Astrud Gilberto also in the 1950s; and in the 1960s, 1970s, and 1980s "Gato" Barbieri, Chick Corea, Ray Barretto, Flora Purim, and several others are much in demand for their mixture of Latin feelings and sounds into their jazz statements.

The very newest thing, called *ju-ju*, is an effort to blend genuine African musical ideas with the traditional Afro-American jazz principles and practices. Where this all will go remains to be seen.

One thing is certain. Jazz is still strong and growing all the time. The black component in American culture has made profound changes in many subtle ways. Henry Pleasants speaks of an Afro-American Epoch in the music of Western Civilization—to take its place in the sequence of Renaissance, Baroque, Classic, Romantic, 20th Century, and Afro-American.[11]. This is heady stuff.

And if Pleasants' provocative remarks were not enough, the U. S. Census Bureau recently released predictions that Hispanic Americans will have passed the black community to become the largest minority group in the nation by the year 2010. And by the year 2080, whites will be a minority group, comprising at that time 46.6% of the population. What this means, of course, is that jazz and the mix of jazz with Latin music will increase in its cultural relevance for American society.

READING NOTES FOR CHAPTER EIGHTEEN

[1]For a full discussion of the criticism jazz received in its early days see Alan Merriam, *The Anthropology of Music* (Chicago: Northwestern University Press, 1964), pp. 241-244.

[2]Charles Keil, *Urban Blues* (Chicago: University of Chicago Press, 1966), p. 12.

[3]The entire Introduction (pp. 1-29) and Chapter I "Afro-American Music" (pp. 30-49) should be required reading in every jazz course taught in America. Nothing published since Keil's book (1966) has changed any of his conclusions. This is a most remarkable analysis of the sociocultural reasons for jazz being what it is.

[4]Keil, *Urban Blues*, *passim*, pp. 6-12.

[5]Keil, *Urban Blues*, pp. 7-8.

[6]LeRoi Jones, *Blues People* (New York: William Morrow, 1963), p. 7.

[7]Keil, *Urban Blues*, p. 20.

[8]The best scholarly examination of black musicians during colonial times and thereafter appears in Eileen Southern, *The Music of Black Americans* (New York: W. W. Norton, 1971).

[9]Among the better books on the blues is Giles Oakley's *The Devil's Music* (New York: Harvest Books, by Harper & Row, Publishers, 1977).

[10]In his *Jazz Piano: History and Development* (Dubuque, Iowa: Wm. C. Brown Company Publishers, 1982), Billy Taylor asserts that jazz is America's classical music. His argument is not entirely convincing as it is stated. What he really means is that jazz is the one musical style which most nearly reveals and reflects that peculiar thing called the American Spirit in all its multi-ethnic diversity.

[11]For a full review of Henry Pleasants' innovative analysis of music in today's society, see *Serious Music—and All That Jazz!* (New York: Simon and Schuster, 1969).

19

Broadway

It is surprising, the number of major stars in entertainment who got their start on Broadway. Many of them started out in other areas, and finally settled into another field, but Broadway, at one time or another, had a major influence in their careers. Fred Astaire, Bob Hope, Al Jolson, Sophie Tucker, Jimmie Durante, right up through Barbra Streisand, and even Linda Ronstadt.

CULTURAL FRAME OF REFERENCE

Sociological Roots

Broadway has been almost the single handed achievement of the Jewish Community on the Eastern Seaboard. With some exceptions, of course, the major innovations and great moments have been the work of urban, sophisticated, upper middle class Jewish leaders in the industry. Many of them were

ILLUSTRATION: Broadway scene. Courtesy of the CCM Publicity Office, Cincinnati, Ohio.

East European immigrants who grew up in poverty circumstances, but soon found their way to stardom and financial security. Irving Berlin, Eddie Cantor, Fanny Brice, and dozens of others got their start when they were mere children. Not only singers and composers, but publishers, producers, arrangers, directors, promoters, agents, and many others behind the scenes had a strong Jewish influence somewhere in their background.

Equally important as the Jewish flavor is, perhaps, the Eastern Seaboard location. Leonard Bernstein once said that Broadway could not have occurred except right in downtown Manhattan. That certain spirit, energy, and mentality just could not have taken form anywhere else in the world.

Psychoemotional Traits

As compared with the folks in Iowa or Wisconsin, the Eastern Seaboard crowd is much more high-strung, brash, brassy, quick witted, verbal, and volatile. Even the cab drivers in New York can discuss things like Norman Mailer's recent works, which bank vice presidents in North Dakota neglect. Animal reflexes of blinding speed are common on the Eastern Coast.

This whole crowd drives toward success and achievement with a singular but realistic thrust. On top, today. On the bottom, tomorrow. So, what else is new? The big question is not, "What have you accomplished?" but "What have you accomplished recently?" This intensity leads to a sometimes shallow and superficial view of life and to emotional and intellectual fatigue, but it also leads to some glorious moments in the arts—like *Porgy and Bess* and *Oklahoma*.

Musical Results

The music—all the way from "Give My Regards to Broadway" to "Hello Dolly" and beyond—reflects and celebrates every nuance of this Eastern Urban Mentality. Broadway musicals are jumpy, nervous, energetic, American splashy, and generally upbeat. Borrowing greatly from European operetta, English beer hall entertainment, the minstrel show, vaudeville, burlesque, and Stephen Foster, and borrowing heavily on black jazz rhythms and harmonies, the American musical became a perfect declaration of that special American character so well known throughout the world.

The music has large doses of syncopated rhythms, slick harmonies, and lovely lingering melodies. It is no accident that Broadway tunes often find their way into the Top Forty popular songs of the mainline pop industry. The tunes are so well wrought and cleverly forthright that they lend themselves to all manner of interpretations by jazz singers, dance band leaders, and night-club entertainers. Indeed, the giant hits of the first half of the 20th Century came, by and large, from Broadway musicals and revues.

Topics of Concern

As might be expected, there are not many Broadway shows about coal mine disasters in the Appalachian Mountains or crop failures in Kansas. Rather, there are many treatments of such Eastern Urban concerns as booze, broads, blades, mistresses, triangles, the rackets, baseball, horses, and city life. The upper class girl falling in love with the lower class boy, or its reverse, and the subsequent moon-June-tune-honeymoon in spite of their parents' violent objections has been a stock formula for a long time, now. Difficulties between cultures or between class levels within the same culture lie at the base of most Broadway shows just as those same difficulties and the resultant misunderstanding provide the basis for most TV sit-coms and comedy routines.

Some of the most charming and effective moments on Broadway have come from the caricatures of typical American figures: the Irish cop, the society matron, the Sugar Daddy, the voluptous blonde, the country bumpkin, and others. In one swift stroke, musical or dramatic, a good Broadway show delivers the instant whole package, the Gestalt, of one of America's kind. In *Oklahoma*, for example, Curly sings to that nasty farmhand, Jud, that if he (Jud) doesn't stop fooling around with Curly's girl, Jud will get himself killed. There will be a big funeral, with lots of people, and everyone singing, "Poor Jud is daid, poor Jud is daid...." And one line in the tune summarizes brilliantly Jud's whole life style and character, "...his fingernails have never been so clean!"

HISTORICAL REVIEW

The Birth of the Genre. Pre-Broadway. Colonial Times to 1904.

The colonial "entertainments," feats of magic wonder, singers, and traveling stage shows blended in later with the English ballad operas, then fed into the minstrel show, vaudeville, burlesque (satire, not strip-tease) routines, and extravaganzas until America was a magnificent mix of musico-theatrical operations. Add to the above a large importation of European operettas and the entire tin-pan alley industry with its traditions and energies—put them all together and something very exciting was bound to happen.

The Baroque Era on Broadway. The Early Years. 1904-1927.

The man who brought it all together—rather like Handel did in the field of classical music—was one of the most dynamic and talented showmen of all time, George M. Cohan. His *Little Johnny Jones* in 1904 set a new and decisive model for things to come. Cohan's musicals were brisk, brassy, breezy, brash, very entertaining, and American to the core. He turned out some 50 musicals, all good, some still the best of the genre. Tunes like "It's a Grand Old Flag" and "I'm a Yankee Doodle Dandy" will last forever.

The Americans instantly recognized this style and spirit as their own. The Broadway musical was born. In a short time Jerome Kern, Irving Berlin, the youthful Cole Porter, and dozens of others were absorbing the nuances and tone, and were pulling their own thoughts and musical energies into line with the new spirit of the times. There were lavish "revues," also: Earl Carroll's *Vanities*, Flo Ziegfeld's *Follies*, and George White's *Scandals*. There were times of Baroque splendor.

The Classic Period on Broadway. Broadway Settles Down 1927-1943.

The early days of Broadway were exciting, filled with a free and spontaneous approach to the theater: beautiful girls, comedy routines, snappy dance numbers, lavish costumes, spectacular sets, the works. Memorable and thrilling. But Jerome Kern (1885-1945) and others began to move away from the accepted cliches and conventions toward a more integrated dramatic whole, with the music used to support and enrich the emotions being generated in the theatrical narrative. After several partially successful early attempts, Kern hit his stride with *Show Boat* (1927).

Show Boat set the course for the growth of the American musical for the next three decades. Here was a solid adult theme, an intense dramatic narrative, a purely American plot, a realistic presentation of something worth talking about. It was too genuinely moving to be confused with operetta or with a revue. It was its own unique thing. *Of Thee I Sing* (George and Ira Gershwin) followed in 1931, and got the Pulitzer Prize for drama. *Porgy and Bess*, a monument in the literature, appeared in 1935. Broadway had settled into a period of full, productive, and virile adulthood.

The Romantic Period on Broadway. Productive Tension. 1943-1960.

The years of World War II and immediately thereafter were filled with activity and energy. Curt Sachs, German musicologist, said in one of his writings that in times of social upheaval—wars, floods, pestilence, earthquakes, plagues, etc.—there is often an outpouring of native creative energies in the arts. Surely this happened in the 40s on Broadway.

Right in the heart of the War, *Oklahoma* appeared. In the center. In the center of America's geographical territory. In the center of America's collective psychoemotional posture. What a remarkable statement of the American way of life. Would any other musical have succeeded at that particular time in America's history—*Funny Girl? Camelot? Company?*

In any case, *Oklahoma* was a superhit, and it proved again, as *Porgy* had proved, that Broadway could handle a powerful topic with depth and sophistication. America now had a musical language, popular music, to match the language and form of the popular theater.

Oklahoma had no traditional chorus girl scenes, but, rather, an extended ballet sequence choreographed by none other than Agnes de Mille. There was a murder scene right on stage, before the audience, and many thought it would never sell. The orchestra was interwoven into the musical and dramatic fabric of the show as never before in a Broadway musical. *Oklahoma* was, in short, another landmark in the development of the American musical theater.

Oscar Hammerstein and Richard Rodgers became a two-man industry. *Carousel* (1945), *South Pacific* (1949), *The King and I* (1951), *Flower Drum Song* (1958), and *The Sound of Music* (1959)—with several lesser successes sprinkled between.

Modern Times. 1960-Present. The Contemporary Scene on Broadway

In addition to the fairly traditional *Funny Girl, Hello Dolly,* and *Fiddler on the Roof,* there have been some not-so-traditional efforts to probe the potential of the American musical theater. *Hair, Oh! Calcutta!, Godspell, Jesus Christ, Superstar,* and others explored the musical idiom of rock for fresh territory. *Applause, Company,* and *A Little Night Music* reach into Freudian self analysis and group encounter activities for their dramatic thrust.

Very common, these days, is for a business conglomerate to put up huge sums of money for the financial launching of a Broadway show—with the show being, in effect, totally owned and controlled all along the way by the conglomerate through its recording company, movie company, and attendant business ties. The refreshing new approach to Broadway, *Best Little Whorehouse in Texas,* is completely owned by Paramount, which is owned by Gulf + Western. For the Paramount movie, the major stars and creative personalities of the original Broadway show were released, and new people brought in. Many songs were dropped, and new ones written by Dolly Parton who had one of the lead roles along with Burt Reynolds. Whatever the artistic merits of the new theatrical piece, now a movie, it is surely much removed from the original work.

While the financial realities of Broadway are, indeed, changing, there is no reason to believe that a good show will not somehow win out. If someone has something to say, and says it with imagination, energy, and precision, the product will sell, in spite of high union labor costs, the porno shops in the theater district, the lack of big name talent, and all the other reasons so often given for the scarcity of superhits. If the message of the show has cultural currency, if the music and dancing are strong, and if the acting is convincing, the work will survive no matter what the critics and scholars might think about it.

There is a brutal beautiful wisdom in the instinctive judgment of "the public." That's the way it should be. They are, after all, the ones for whom the arts are intended.

Just recently a most unlikely topic drew Andrew Lloyd Webber back to musical theater, cats. Yes, with lyrics from obscure poems by T. S. Eliot, Webber has created a stunning Broadway show called *Cats*. The public acceptance of the show has been one of the surprises of the 1982-1983 theater season. "Memory," a song taken from the show, has been recorded by Barry Manilow (among others) and looks to be one of the big show tunes of the 80s.

Country Music

Country music is the most misunderstood and maligned music in the business. Its critics are brutal in their sweeping discrimination against it, and honestly believe it to be an affront to basic music sensibilities. Its producers and consumers are almost paranoid in their defensive attitude, and honestly believe it is the only decent and pure thing left in America.

It is, of course, neither. It is the musical behavior of a certain crowd of people with certain characteristics.

CULTURAL FRAME OF REFERENCE

Sociological Roots

Country music comes out of an Anglo-Celtic Protestant culture which derives from the British Isles. The Anglo-Celtic (Welsh, Irish Gaelic, and Scottish Gaelic) spirit is slightly more individualistic and high-strung than the malleable Anglo-Saxon mentality, and accounts for a certain noticeable brand of

ILLUSTRATION: Hank Williams, Jr. Courtesy of Elektra Records.

189

stubborn pride and almost hostile independence. These folks settled in the mountains of Appalachia, in the adjacent flat lands, and in the tidewater backwoods country across the Southeastern and South Central United States. After many generations of separation from the mainstream of American society on the Eastern Seaboard, the then only modest genetic difference took on increased depth and strength until this whole geographic area became a distinctly different crowd from their Anglo-Saxon shopkeeping ancestors and relatives in Boston and Philadelphia. The economics of the rural-agrarian South being as isolationalistic as it was, this genetic difference produced, over the years, a prolonged history of ignorance, poverty, disease, and cultural fatigue. Country music's most respected scholar-historian, Bill C. Malone, is very matter-of-fact.

> The socially ingrown rural South, from the tidewater of Virginia to the pine barrens of East Texas, produced a population that, in its commitment to and preservation of traditional cultural values should be considered as a distinct family unit.

> The music of these people, lying outside the main-stream of American cultural development, provided the origin and nucleus of what we now call country music.[1]

In the 30s and 40s and 50s, when they moved to the cities in search of a better life, the Appalachians could not make the adjustment to factory whistles, and street car tracks, and crowded sidewalks, and asphalt playgrounds. They ended up broken in spirit, sick, and on welfare. The Appalachian ghettos of Detroit, Chicago, Cincinnati, and Boston are very real yet today.

Psychoemotional Traits

The Appalachians are a fiercely independent lot, with deep traditional views of reality.[2] They are fearful and suspicious of intellectual abstractions. They think in specific yet imaginative language. Country tunes are filled with colorful and catchy lyrics. Broadway lyrics are imaginative, too, of course, but the country tunes have that home-spun texture to them.

190

The folks who produce and consume country music are extremely loyal and strong in their friendships. During the Second World War, the Chrysler Corporation, Willow Run, Michigan, had a lot of trouble finding foremen and section leaders for the aircraft engine assembly lines. The Appalachians had migrated from the South to Willow Run and other industrial areas in the North, and they made good workers, by and large. But they did not want to take positions of leadership or authority for fear that they would lose their friends working along side them on the assembly line.

The whole Appalachian community is very definitely person oriented, not thing oriented or achievement oriented. "A man's a man, and that's all! Makes no matter how many fancy words he kin talk!" Millionaire songwriter Merle Haggard still drinks whiskey and goes fishing with some of the old cronies he had before he made it big.

Person oriented. Not time oriented. Not locked into the hours-and-weeks goal drive concept of time held by middle class Americans. No appointment books and calendar schedules in the hills of Appalachia, or in the depths of the Appalachian ghetto of Detroit. Jack Weller, a Presbyterian minister in the mountains for 10 years or more, tells about trying to get some men lined up to paint the church. He went around to all the mountain homes trying to get the men to commit themselves for a specific Saturday morning's work. He could not get a single mountaineer to say he would work on a given Saturday. Things might come up. Never know what a man might be doing a month from now. Better not plan on it.

Finally, in frustration, the Reverend Weller simply went out and bought a dozen buckets of paint and a dozen brushes, put them on the front porch of the church, and sat down by himself to wait until the mountain men would come by the church on their way to the general store for weekly supplies. As the men came by the church, Weller called out to ask if they might grab a brush and "paint a spell." Sure enough. Several of the men painted a spell, then sat and visited a spell, then painted a spell more. In a few days Weller got the entire church painted by catching passers-by. These same men, however, would not commit themselves in advance for any painting duty.[3]

191

Time is different. Time is an endless unfolding of a long range pattern. Tomorrow is probably going to be pretty much like yesterday; and last year was not much different from the year before. The crop failures, the mountain slides, the coal mine disasters, the good times and the bad times come and go, but things really don't change all that much.

Musical Results

What kind of music springs from this basic approach to life? A music which is open and unashamedly simple and emotional. The music reflects the attitudes cherished in the culture: direct and straight forward remarks about things which are now, and have always been, part of the human condition.

The melodies are relatively short and predictable. The harmonies are few and conventional. The rhythms are simple and traditional. The forms are closed in non-architectural designs. The whole musical art is a rather transparent declaration of a rather transparent approach to life, love, truth, beauty, justice, and all the rest. Transparent, yes; but now shallow. This is a deep and clean transparency, like a spring-fed mountain lake.

Topics of Concern

The topics are pretty straight forward, too. At least five major areas get worked over and over again, year after year.

(1) Religious and patriotic statements arise from firm beliefs about the virtues of God and Country. Porter Wagoner steps forward near the end of his Saturday 5:30 TV show, and says, "And now, folks, here's our hymn for tonight." He then swings into a country version of "What a Friend We Have in Jesus." Merle Haggard still gets requests for "Okie from Muskogee," years after the Viet Nam War has lost all its emotional urgency. The tune still represents a certain definite approach to America, and this approach is what gets celebrated each time.

(2) Troubles with prison and the law establishment have been part of country music since its earliest days. The Appalachian has always had trouble interpreting and adhering to middle class laws on drinking, hunting, income tax, license tags,

public school regulations, installment contracts, legal papers, and dozens of technicalities about how a man can or cannot live. Jail house and prison songs are thus big in the business.

(3) Problems adjusting to middle class technological-industrial ways run through country music, also. In the old days, it was mine disasters and railroads. Now the honky-tonking city life and the seven-days-on-the-road trucking industry create the unhappiness. Over and over again the songs speak of heartaches and sorrow and humiliation in the face of technological wonders not understood or favored, and of yearning to be back in the beautiful hills on a little piece of ground where a man can call his soul his own. The dream is imperfect, of course, but the theme is consistent.

(4) Love, death, family ties, marriage, children, kin folk, and the whole battery of the entangling emotions of the matri-patriarchal web get full treatment in country music. In a way which would embarrass a middle class office worker, the singers deliver what are known as "country weepers" in the trade. Flat out, tear jerking, "D-I-V-O-R-C-E" spelled Tammy Wynette in her early career, and the whole country music industry grieved right along with her. Many years later, Kenny Rogers complained that Lucille left him with four hungry children and crops to be taken in. Could that theme possibly have been delivered with a straight face by Frank Sinatra, or Rod Stewart, or Al Jarreau?

(5) Whiskey and wild women balance the scale, lest anyone think that all country music is about purity and goodness. The distinct realization that he is imperfect and subject to temptation flows through the country singer's song repertory, all the way from "I'm a Honky Tonk Man" to "Corn Liquor." "Back Street Affair" and "Your Cheating Heart" were big hits because they touched on a subject still rather delicate in the culture.

Divorce, drinking, cheating, and such things lost their potency on the Eastern Seaboard many years ago, but in country music the topics are still capable of generating some interest. As country music moves into the mainstream of American entertainment, the topics are changing rapidly, though. Dolly Parton's recent lament about harassment,

"Nine to Five", is a significant shift from coal mine disasters and train wrecks.

HISTORICAL REVIEW

The Birth of the Genre. Colonial Times to 1920.

Country music was buried in the hills for a long time. Anglo-Celtic communities dotted the colonial map all the way from Eastern Canada and New England to Virginia and the Carolina tidewater area deep into the Appalachian Mountains. These folks absorbed mainstream American ways very slowly since they were so isolated from the other colonial territories. Even today, there are occasional pockets of near Elizabethan culture discovered in the mountains.

The Baroque Era. Commercial Recognition. 1920-1930.

With the development of records and radio as national entertainment media, country music suddenly became a commercial commodity to be marketed and sold for profit. Ralph Peer (Okeh Records) and other recording executives hurried from New York down South to record the likes of Jimmie Rodgers (1897-1933), Fiddlin' John Carson (1868-1949), and others. The Carter Family—Alvin P. (1891-1960), his wife Sarah (1898-1974), and his brother's wife Maybelle (1909-1982)—became one of the most influential of all country music pioneer groups.

The National Barn Dance, sponsored by Sears and Roebuck over the company owned radio station in Chicago ("World's Largest Store" thus station W L S), brought a host of entertainers into national prominence—George Goebel, Fibber McGee and Molly, Gene Autry, and many others. Another barn dance appeared shortly thereafter in Nashville. This, too, was sponsored by a big company, the National Life and Accident Insurance Company, and promoted over its own radio station ("We Shield Millions" thus station W S M). The show turned into the Grand Ole Opry a few years later, and the rest is history.

Soon, all the major recording companies had a special series of records devoted to "songs of the hills and plains,"

Columbia's 15000-D series, for example, and a special set of numbers in Victor's Bluebird label. Okeh Records used the term "old-time music." The big mail order houses did a high volume business in country music during the early days.

Vernon Dalhart (1883-1948) (real name Marion Try Slaughter), had a big hit in 1924, "The Prisoner's Song." A trained singer who had appeared in Dallas in Puccini's "Girl of the Golden West," Dalhart nonetheless reached his greatest fame as a singer of country tunes.

These were colorful and flamboyant days. The music was produced mostly by string instruments, the songs were pure mountain-style declarations, and the musicians were untutored originals with a gift for memorable names: Gid Tanner and the Skillet Lickers, The Carolina Tar Heels, Dr. Humphrey Bate and the Possum Hunters, The Gully Jumpers, and the Fruit Jar Drinkers.

The Classic Period in Country Music.
The Cowboy Influence. 1930-1940.

With the great migration of people out of the Southeast to the North and West, and with the enormous social upheaval from the Great Depression and the dust bowl tragedies, a host of sociocultural exchanges occurred which threw Southeast style country music into contact with the Southwest style country music (already a rich mixture of Southern white, cotton slave Black, Mexican, Louisiana Cajun, and others).

The musical and social base was there, to be sure, but the man who almost single-handedly combined the fields was none other than America's first real cowboy hero, Gene Autry. Autry was no more a cowboy than any other worker at the railroad telegraph station in Sapulpa, Oklahoma. And during the first few years of his enormous success on the WLS Barn Dance in Chicago, he sang regular country tunes. His "cowboy image" was a later creation of the Hollywood studios, Republic and Monogram. It paid off, and brought in a whole new age to the pop arts in America. Tex Ritter, Roy Rogers, Bob Nolan and the Sons of the Pioneers. Glorious days of Americana.

While the cowboy thing was growing, and bringing into existence the term "Country and Western Music," Roy Acuff and others went right on singing about coal mine disasters and the Smokey Mountains at daybreak. Bill Monroe, too, was not much interested in cowboy music. He was carving out a new thing called Blue Grass. With Lester Flatt and Earl Scruggs working in his group, Monroe launched a subdivision of country music which has become a whole art in itself.

The classic Blue Grass group consists of mandolin, 5-string banjo, guitar, fiddle, and string bass. More recent groups might have a pedal steel guitar, an amplified bass guitar, and drums. The real heart of Blue Grass is the intricate banjo picking. Whatever else might accrue to it, the art of Blue Grass will draw on that ricka-chicka-ricka-chicka hypnotic 5-string banjo.

Another thing that happened in the 1930s was the rise of "Western Swing" mostly under the leadership of Bob Wills and his Texas Playboys. With Benny Goodman and Tommy Dorsey of middle class America so big on the scene, it was only natural that someone would try the same approach in country music. Bob Wills had 15 pieces in his band in 1938. Saxophones, violins, drums, piano, amplified steel guitar, amplified rhythm guitar, string bass—the works. The musical product was a cross between Roy Acuff and Glenn Miller. Very interesting and profitable. Wills caused a major crisis at the Grand Ole Opry when he refused to perform without his drummer. The Opry officials had never had drums on the show, and were not about to give in. Wills and the officials argued for a while, then finally compromised by putting Wills' drummer behind a curtain so he would be hidden from the audience's view—but Wills could still hear the beat he needed for his performance style.

The Romantic Period in Country Music.
Country Music Goes Public. 1940-1955.

The Second World War sent boys from Maine into army camps in Mississippi, and country kids from West Virginia into camps in California. It also moved thousands of defense plant workers all over the nation, and led to explosive growth in the trucking industry. Workers male and female poured out of the South to find jobs in Detroit, Chicago, Los Angeles, and

Boston. They brought their guitars and their musical tastes with them.

The invention of the 45 r.p.m. record enabled small independent recording companies to challenge the giants by filling up the back seat of a station wagon with records and posters, and hustling up a good week's profit between Chicago, Memphis, Detroit, and Cincinnati. These little record companies signed on a good number of country musicians who had been ignored by the giants on the Eastern Seaboard.

Fred Rose broke away from ASCAP (The American Society of Composers, Authors and Publishers), and with Roy Acuff launched not only his own Acuff-Rose Publishing Company, but also worked to promote the formation of BMI (Broadcast Music, Inc.), a rival performance rights licensing organization. ASCAP had pretty much ignored the country market, and BMI found itself with more talent than it had even guessed might be around.

The result of all these developments in the industry was the penetration of country music into the heart of mainstream American musical tastes. Eddy Arnold, Ernie Ford, Hank Williams, and many others were "accepted" by middle class America as Lulla Belle and Scotty had never been. It was still country music, of course, but Hank Williams' tunes were played and sung by everyone from Bing Crosby to the Boston Pops.

Patti Page put an uninspired ditty on the B-side of a 1950 release, and found herself with, as Wesley Rose (Fred's son) has said, "The first song ever to be No. 1 in every civilized nation on the globe: The Tennessee Waltz." This tune did not hurt the country music industry at all.

Modern Country Music. The Big Time. 1955-present.

With Elvis Presley, Bill Haley, Jerry Lee Lewis, Carl Perkins, and others, country music entered a short period of trauma and indecision. Many people thought the new rock 'n' roll would be the end of genuine country music. Harold Jenkins changed his name to Conway Twitty and launched out on a rock 'n' roll career. He's back in country music, again, and doing very well. Charlie Rich labored in the fields of jazz and blues, and he, too, is back in country music.

The crisis was short-lived, and Elvis took the field of rock 'n' roll off into 32 movies, millions of records, and a whole world of things not at all related to Prince Albert Pipe Tobacco and the Smokey Mountains at daybreak.

Then, during Elvis' two years in the service, a new crowd of country musicians began to assert themselves. Many were veterans of the country music business who actually profited by the interest in Elvis and Buddy Holly and other rockabilly artists. By the 1960s Nashville had become the center of the industry.

> The city's 40 [recording] studies produce more 45 rpm or "single" records than any city in the world. In Nashville there are more than 1,500 union musicians and an equal number of songwriters, served by 29 talent agencies, seven record-pressing plants, 400 music publishing houses, 53 record companies, offices for three performing-rights organizations, and seven trade papers.

These figures are probably double that now. Hemphill was writing in the late 1960s.

Earlier, in 1962, a startling thing happened. Ray Charles, a black, blind, blues singer went right into the heart of what had been this pure white country music mecca, and recorded a tune written by country songwriter Don Gibson, "I Can't Stop Lovin' You." Produced by Sid Feller, with the orchestra and chorus conducted by jazzman Marty Paich, the recording sold enormously well in both the black and white country, and even the white middle-class, markets.

About the time of Watergate, the entire world of popular music took a turn toward new directions, country music included. Of course. That's what popular music—and country music had now become one of the big categories in America's popular music industry—is all about: an instant and direct index into the collective stirrings of American society-at-large.

And America was surely different now. The Viet Nam War was ended. Richard Nixon, the highest political figure in all Western Civilization, resigned from office. The racial militants who had been trying to burn down the university computer center in the 1960s were now getting their hair cut and putting on shoes and looking for work. It was the end of one age, and the careful beginning of another. This new age would be a little laid back.

As country musicians moved toward the center of mainstream America, they inevitably picked up the appropriate traits. The music became less and less nasal, more and more open. Chords, melodies, rhythms, instruments—everything. The intermixing and interlacing of different musical styles has led to a number of general categories.

(1) Pop-Country. Some critics say it's all become pop-country. Not really. There is still a noticeable difference between Tanya Tucker and Barbra Streisand. A big field does exist, here, though. Barbara Mandrell, Glenn Campbell, and others have become pop singers in every conception of the term. Their subjects may or may not have a decided country ring. Their voices do not specifically brand them as country singers. Their careers are very much pop oriented in every direction.

(2) Mainstream Country. In the steady progression from the 1920s to the present, country music has become quite modern. Drums, dozens of microphones, banks of speakers, electric pianos, everything amplified. In this mainstream line of development would be Loretta Lynn, Conway Twitty, Merle Haggard, Mel Tillis, Porter Wagoner, early Dolly Parton, and many others. It's country music all the way, but rather modern in comparison with Mother Maybelle Carter.

(3) Old Timey Country. A big industry, yet. Fiddles, banjos, raw-boned nasal singers, week-end festivals in Virginia. Jean Ritchie and all her associates are very much alive and well in this area.

(4) Country Rock. Early Linda Ronstadt and Skeeter Davis, recently. The early Eagles. Alabama. And that special group of outlaws branded by *Time* magazine as the Redneck Rock crowd—Waylon Jennings, Willie Nelson, and convicted killer David Allen Coe. There are some music scholars who predict that the next big figure—the next Bob Dylan or the next Beatles—will come out of the field of Redneck Rock.

(5) Blue Grass. Still very big, and growing. The "New Grass" groups as they are sometimes called feature drums, amplified instruments, and other accoutrements foreign to old-

time blue grass, but the general style is very clearly in the line of traditional blue grass.

(6) Jazz Flavored Country Music. David Grisman plays a cross between blue grass and jazz which he calls "dawg music." He has recorded with Stephane Gappelli, the well known jazz violinist, and the public seems to be attracted to the new music.

Something new may be on the way. A new group, Cowboy Jazz, plays just that—a jazz based kind of Sons of the Pioneers music with great appeal. The result is surprisingly refreshing in its infectious enthusiasm.

One thing is certain. Country music is certainly in the big leagues, now. It has become a multi-million dollar enterprise, and it shows some remarkable similarities to jazz when jazz was at its popular peak. Folks dance to country music these days—just like they used to go out to a big night club to dance to jazz bands. Monday night is "jam night" at many of the big clubs featuring country music—just like in the old days when "jamming" (bringing your instrument to "sit in" with the house band) was a favorite jazz social ritual. And the major singers are moving their musical careers into acting and film work—just like Doris Day, Betty Grable, Frank Sinatra, and other big band singers moved into acting and films.

Whatever happens to country music, it will probably hang on to a certain aesthetic core which gives it that special tang. There is something unique about it. It has a peculiar feel to it. Jazz went through a lot, but there is still a particular something that has remained through all the various style changes. Country music, too, is so strong that it will undoubtedly survive all overt and covert efforts to delete or dilute its contribution to the American musical environment.

READING NOTES FOR CHAPTER TWENTY

[1]The quotation and the previous paragraphs are drawn from Bill C. Malone, *Country Music U. S. A.* (Austin, Texas: The University of Texas Press, 1968), Introduction and p. 5.

[2]Although it has been criticized for its sweeping generalizations, still the best book for understanding the pronounced differences between mountain culture and WASP culture is Jack E. Weller, *Yesterday's People: Life in Contemporary Appalachia* (Lexington, Kentucky: University of Kentucky Press, 1950). Most of Weller's observations are confirmed in a study of country music.

[3]Weller, *Yesterday's People*, pp. 42-43.

[4]Paul Hemphill, *The Nashville Sound,* (New York: Simon and Schuster, 1970), p. 11.

21

Rock

It may seem a bit presumptuous, academically, to rank the young field of rock along with jazz, classical music, and the others. It would be presumptuous, most assuredly, if rock were just a temporary style. But it is not temporary, it is new culture. The culture is constantly changing, of course, but it is strong and distinct.

CULTURAL FRAME OF REFERENCE

Sociological Roots

Rock comes out of a revolution of the deepest kind. A revolution of middle class white Anglo-Saxon and Jewish youngsters who rejected nothing less than the very foundation of Western Civilization, Progress. What started out as an innocent hip-swinging version of "Blue Suede Shoes," soon turned into a genuine revolution by the time it got to San Francisco, Woodstock, and Altamont.

ILLUSTRATION: AC/DC's Angus Young and Brian Johnson. Courtesy of Atlantic Records.

While parents and religious leaders thought it was the work of the evil forces in society, Margaret Mead observed that it was simply a quick shift from a post-figurative culture (parents set the norms) to co-figurative culture (parents and children work out norms together) to a pre-figurative culture (youngsters set the behavior norms while the elders try to catch and hang on to the reality of the day). All this happened from the early 1940s to the late 1960s, and America went through some fitfully sleepless nights.

McLuhan observed that such revolutionary things always happen when a society moves from one major sensory medium to another—in this case, from a long-standing visual print culture to a tactile aural electronic tribal culture.

Psychoemotional Traits

The young people of the 1950s and 1960s felt that the society they were about to enter was seriously flawed in several areas, but especially in political and business matters. They rejected the notion that a certain amount of greed and corruption was just normal. They were absolutely furious with politicians and businessmen who supported the Viet Nam War with their speeches, chemicals, and military hardware.

This generation of the "baby boom" wanted to get off the middle class achievement treadmill. They wanted to explore life in depth, and they felt that traditional society was too "one dimensional." Therefore they tried to expand their consciousness with drugs, meditation, Oriental philosophy, and similar unorthodox techniques. They were cynical, disillusioned, and disenchanted with reason, committees, technology, and political compromise as the solutions to society's needs.

These young people had little patience with traditional patterns of deferred gratification. They wanted action. Now. Tomorrow was never. This was an age of Instant Everything.

Musical Results

The search for deep, honest, authentic music to declare themselves led the rock crowd to go right around Count Basie, Julie Andrews, Perry Como, and Duke Ellington. Right around the sophisticated high-gloss music Establishment—back, instead, to the most primitive stuff they could find: Leadbelly, Lightnin' Hopkins, Mother Maybelle Carter. To the two most honest and untarnished fields of music they could find, black music and country music.

Away with the controlled and conventional music making. The Now Generation moved toward an exploitation of all possible unorthodox melodies, harmonies, forms, sounds, and stage techniques. For the Grateful Dead, music was Experience. And the San Francisco Psychedelic Scene turned to multi-media and multi-sensory environments for music.

In strict musical terms, the new music simplified things. Gone were the elaborate complexities of be-bop and the big swing bands. Now things were stripped down to bare essentials. Triads rather than ninth chords and eleventh chords. Direct leaps from one key to another, rather than clever modulations. Eighth note rhythmic feeling was everywhere, rather than the dotted eighth and sixteenth so common in previous days. The times, indeed, were a changing.

Topics of Concern

The revolution is over, and the most hostile former revolutionaries are now coaching Little League Baseball, are active in the PTA, and are selling real estate. Even Jerry Rubin is a stock broker in New York. And Jane Fonda is a very successful business woman.

In their day, at their peak, the revolutionaries rejected everything the Establishment held dear: religion, government, family, authority, achievement, linear thinking, educational goals, everything. Especially pollution, poverty, corruption, war, and inhuman social conditions as the price society has to pay for Progress. The kids were a little disorganized at times, but they launched a brutal four-letter attack on all the surface propriety of the conventional way of American life.

HISTORICAL PERSPECTIVE

The Birth of the Genre. Rhythm and Blues. 1940-1954.

In *Honkers and Shouters*, Arnold Shaw's masterful introduction, "Anatomy of Rhythm and Blues," shows clearly that rock owes it major musical spirit and style to the black race records which *Billboard* began to call Rhythm and Blues in 1949. In all its essential features, early rock 'n' roll is simply white rhythm and blues. Elvis Presley's debt to Big Boy Crudup and Big Bill Broonzy is well documented, now, but not many musicians or fans knew it when Elvis first appeared on the scene.

The musical style goes all the way back to Bessie Smith and the early blues singers, of course, but the unique commercial feeling of rhythm and blues is a product of the juke box which so dominated things in popular music immediately after World War II. All that was needed was a white industry to market the product. That industry, and its super salesmen, the disc jockeys, blossomed and bore diverse fruits of astonishing financial gain when Elvis finally rose to cult hero status.

The Baroque Era. Elvis and the Rockabillies. 1954-1958.

Elvis was a perfect, ready-made anti-Establishment figure. All that black hair, the suggestion of sex which came from the crooked smile, no education, no musical refinement—but he loved his mom, grew up in the church, and always said, "Yes, Sir," to the reporters. His synthesis of country music and black music caught on, to say the least. And Elvis was a Baroque character if there ever was one.

The war babies were now 9-11 years old, the radio age. Top-40 Radio Programming replaced traditional programming. The disc jockey rose to heights of strange power, and he became a teen hero.

The 45 r.p.m. record gave little independent companies a chance to challenge the giants, and they did. The 45 r.p.m. turned out to be ideal for rock 'n' roll. It was the dawn of a new age, an age of Chess Records, Jubilee Records, Sun Records, and many others reaching out into the new teen market.

The Classic Period. American Bandstand. 1958-1964.

The big record companies discovered the money to be made in this new rock 'n' roll genre, and they moved in. The Everly Brothers left Cadence to sign with Warner Brothers, and Bob Dylan signed with Columbia. Chubby Checker made "The Twist" famous. Hootenannies became popular on television. Chuck Berry, the pure rock 'n' roll artist, was at his peak.

Dick Clark survived the payola hearings in Congress, and his American Bandstand was more popular than ever. The war babies were in their middle and late teens, now, and rock 'n' roll was in its purest, relatively non-political, classic age.

The Romantic Period. The British Invasion and San Francisco. 1964-1974.

The Beatles. The Rolling Stones. The San Francisco Psychedelic Scene. The Jefferson Airplane. The Grateful Dead. And that most Romantic of all rock 'n' roll events: Woodstock. By this time, the term had been shortened, and the music was called just rock. The term rock 'n' roll, when used, was used to refer to innocent days gone by when the music was cute and light. The new rock was not cute, not light. It was terribly serious business.

The whole musical matrix got stretched in all directions —melody, harmony, rhythm, instrumentation, synthesizers, ring modulators, the works. Acid rock. Psychedelic rock. Multi-media, multi-sensory, simultaneous bombardment of the senses at the threshhold of pain. The war babies were in their early 20s now, and capable of some frightening and imaginatively dangerous explorations into mind stretching experiences.

The record now became the primary aesthetic experience, to be listened to with stereo headphones. The concerts were mere celebration rituals. No one went to Woodstock to hear music. They took that religious pilgrimage for other reasons, mostly as a declaration of faith in the communal belief that the Establishment way of doing things was wrong, and they would offer a new alternative. The musical presentations were really secondary to the central purpose of the event.

The act of recording became the compositional act, too, with the mixing board being critical. Rock groups went into the recording studio with a general feeling of what they wanted to accomplish. The infinite changes, adjustments, additions, deletions, over dubbing, and such were often more creative than the original basic idea. The results were sometimes weak, but sometimes very very strong. The Beatles' *Sgt. Pepper* album brought "composing in the studio" to a new artistic peak.

Modern Times. 1974-Present.

By the time Watergate brought about Richard Nixon's resignation in August of 1974, the world of rock had suffered the loss of Janis Joplin and Jimi Hendrix (both in 1970), waves of campus unrest, the disbanding of the Beatles, and a host of political changes brought about by the beginning of the end of the Viet Nam War. Bob Dylan made a comeback in 1974, but failed to generate the fierce loyalties he once did. The times had changed. Cultural fatigue had set in.

Several musical meteors flashed across the rock horizon —disco, punk, new wave, reggae, salsa, and others. The war babies are now in their middle and late 30s and they are in the work market, nine to five, with less time on their hands and less inclination to bounce from one musical style to another. Things are slowing down, a little. The Flower Children are now firmly lodged in Establishment law firms, school systems, insurance companies, and big corporations. Levi Strauss has come out with a new style of jeans, with a little more room in the seat and thigh, for the changing male body ravaged by, as *Time* magazine said, the effects of roast beef and gravity.

Several major areas of musical behavior are clearly evident. Some writers have called this the age of hyphenated rock.

Pop-rock is a term used to refer to that middle of the road music which has mellowed out of the earlier aggressive and abrasive rock. Elton John. Barry Manilow. Carole King. It is really a new kind of Tin Pan Alley. Donny and Marie Osmond have developed a style out of the rock musical idiom, and it is essentially a popular kind of music. Dozens of others have done likewise.

Country-rock superstars, The Eagles, have now disbanded, but the group gave country-rock a firm place in the pop music of the land in their early years. Alabama has replaced The Eagles as the most popular group in the style. Willie Nelson and Waylon Jennings, with their special brand of outlaw lyrics, carry the style these days. *Urban Cowboy* gave the music a film coverage which popularized the mechanical bull in country night clubs all over the land. With Barbara Mandrell and Kenny Rogers, the style shows all signs of vigorous health.

Jazz-rock, fusion, as it is often called, seems to have been given a sense of direction with Miles Davis landmark recording, *Bitches Brew*, in 1969. Guitarist Al DiMeola, bassist Jaco Pastorius, and pianist Bob James have embraced the more sophisticated techniques of jazz and rock to deliver a mixture of considerable musical interest and excitement.

Nostalgic rock, led by Sha Na Na, reproduces the spirit and style of the early days of the doo-wop groups out of the projects in New York and Los Angeles. *Happy Days* captures that whole feeling on TV, as did *Grease* on film.

Heavy Metal, still around in groups like Van Halen and Judas Priest, survives in full strength and amplitude even though many people in the industry predict its passing any day now.

Punk and New Wave, not the same at all among those who know, but often thrown together, caused quite a stir in the late 1970s with a two-pronged diatribe against middle class society and the rock Establishment. Both British and American rock went through an intense period of hostility, alienation, and violence along with bizarre dress, wierd hair styles, and obscene lyrics.

Techo-rock, a term used by the Wall Street Journal, describes a rather phenomenon sweeping through the Eastern Seaboard clubs—old fashioned songs about normal things, but done up in synthesizers, electronci drums, computer governed instruments, and related technological wonders.

Where does all this eventually go? It goes wherever society takes it. Music is a manifestation of the deepest stirrings in the collective breast of the culture. Among the 70 million or more babies born between 1946 and 1964, the world of rock expresses their attitudes and feelings more succinctly and with greater force than any of the other available genres in the land.

EPILOGUE

What does it all mean? As one of my students said recently, "I took your course last year; got straight A's; loved it. But I still don't like classical music. Where did we fail?"

My response was simple. "We didn't fail. The idea was not to get you to *like* classical music, or any other kind of music, but to *appreciate* music." The name of the course is Music Appreciation—not Music Fondness, or Music Liking, or The Enjoyment of Music.

If a science teacher delivers a unit on the trees of North America, and at the end of the unit a student still doesn't like birch trees, has the course failed? Of course not. The purpose of a college course is not, and should not be, to get you to "like" or "dislike" anything, but rather to get you to see how the subject fits into the broad scheme of human affairs and, perhaps, how you might make use of your new-found awareness to bring a little greater breadth and depth to your life.

The purpose of this book, *The Musical Imperative*, is to suggest how music works in the life of humankind, to stimulate some new thinking about America's major musical genres. There is an abundance of high quality music "out there," and its all readily available through radio, tapes, and recordings. Don't be upset by the great diversity. Take joy in the happiness all these various musical styles bring to their listeners.

This is an unusual music appreciation book. It is not a textbook in the traditional manner, but rather a kind of road map through musical territory which is often fairly well known to both teachers and students. What I really wanted to write, and I'm not sure I have succeeded, is something between *Cliffs Notes* and the big elaborate books by Machlis, Hickok, and others.

Having completed the book, several conditions should have changed. One, you now understand a little more clearly how music is put together—melodies, harmonies, etc. Two, you now understand how music derives from different attitudes held by the different subcultures in America. Three, you can now compare Baroque, Classic, and Romantic tendencies in several musical genres.

Four, and most important of all, you are now less hostile toward certain kinds of music than you were before. That is, you *appreciate* some genres of music even if you are not really fond of them.

If the above conditions do now obtain, we have all been winners. We see, and hear, and understand more clearly what was previously a little unclear. This is, and should be, what education is all about.

INDEX

213

INDEX (continued)

INDEX (continued)

INDEX (continued)

216

INDEX (continued)

INDEX (continued)

INDEX (continued)

INDEX (continued)

Consonant harmony, 41
Constantinople, 156
Continuo, 81
Contrabassoon, 66
Contralto, 99
Contrapuntal forms, 55
Contrast, 158
Control, 16, 163
Cool School, 165, 175
Copland, Aaron, 4, 40, 162
  Outdoor Overture, 86
  Rodeo Ballet Suite, 79
Copyist, 127
Copyright lawyers, 128
Corea, Chick, 59, 178
"Corn Liquor," 193
Cornet, 64
Corporations, 208
Corruption, 205
Costume designers, 127
Costumes, 184
Cotillion Records, 77
Council of Trent, 156
Counter-melody, 43, 55
Counterpoint, 156
Countertenor voice, 101
Country (God andCountry), 152, 192
Country and Western, 9, 67
Country blues, 12, 170
Country bumpkin, 183
Country music, 7, 9, 16, 25, 146, 153, 189-200
"Country Roads," 42
Country voices, 96
Country weepers, 193
Country-rock, 199, 209
Courante, 74
Cowboy Jazz (musical group), 200
Cowboy movie, 11
Credo, 139

Crescendo, 23
Crew Cuts (musical group), 106
Crop failures, 183, 192
Crosby, Bing, 9, 45, 97, 98, 173, 181, 197
Crosby, Bob, 169
  Bobcats, 174
Crosby, Stills, and Nash (musical group), 79
  Suite: Judy Blue Eyes, 79
Cross flutes, 64
Cross rhythms, 37
"Crown of Creation," 30
Crudup, Big Boy, 206
Cubism, 5, 161
Cui, Cesar, 160
Cultural conditioning, 4
Cultural currency, 13
Cultural frame of reference, 145
Cultural imperative, 13
Culturally conditioned response, 4
Culture
  vocabulary of, 5
Cymbal, 63
Czechs, 160

Da Vinci, Leonardo, 156
Dadaism, 161
Dalhart, Vernon, 195
Dallas, Texas, 195
Dance band musicians, 154, 183
"Dance of the Athletes," 10
Dance tunes, 74, 184
Dancing, 168, 187
Darwin, Charles, 22, 152
David, Hal, 30
Davis, Miles, 41, 44, 45, 87, 209
  Bitches Brew, 177, 209
Davis, Skeeter, 199
Dawg music, 200
Day, Doris, 98, 200

220

INDEX (continued)

INDEX (continued)

INDEX (continued)

INDEX (continued)

INDEX (continued)

INDEX (continued)

INDEX (continued)

INDEX (continued)

INDEX (continued)

INDEX (continued)

INDEX (continued)

INDEX (continued)

INDEX (continued)

INDEX (continued)

INDEX (continued)

INDEX (continued)

Index Prepared
by
Warren J. Anderson